Praise for *Perfect*

"*Perfect* is a powerful and engaging story that invites readers to embrace their true greatness as they let go of limiting thoughts that no longer serve them. As readers take this journey with Judi Miller, they witness how fear can be transformed into love. Judi masterfully shows us that we live in a loving and supportive Universe and that the path to happiness begins with opening our hearts and trusting the divine guidance that lives within us all. This is a must read."

Sonia Choquette
Celebrated author of twenty-seven international
best-selling books including *New York Times*
bestseller *The Answer is Simple*

"Now more than ever is the time for us to awaken to the truth of who we are and what we are actually capable of creating with our lives here on earth. In her profound work, *Perfect*, Judi Miller has tapped into what matters most and presented it in a manner that everyone can easily receive and awaken through. Judi shows us skillfully that our life experience is a projected illusion and that we can actually shape shift our reality with the tools of forgiveness and self-liberation. Most importantly, she shows us how. This is a must read for anyone who wants to transform their life and awaken to their true creatorship. Thank you, Judi!"

Dr. Sue Morter
Founder of Morter Institute for Bio-Energetics
Author of #1 *Los Angeles Times* best-selling book *The Energy Codes*
Host of *Healing Matrix* on Gaia TV

"*Perfect* is a book that will open your eyes to a realm of new possibilities. By embracing these simple yet powerful concepts, you are invited to a whole new way of living where a path filled with more possibility, passion, and joy awaits you. It doesn't get any better than that!"

Janet Bray Attwood
New York Times best-selling author of
The Passion Test and *Your Hidden Riches*

"In *Perfect*, Judi Miller masterfully brings us along on her journey from an accounting professional with an inexplicable fear of the dark to a profoundly enlightened human with direct experiences of the perfection of the Universe. With her exquisite prose, Miller manages to touch us deeply while giving us insights as to why we are here on earth and how we can heal generations by opening our hearts."

Debra Poneman
Founder and President, Yes to Success, Inc.

"This is an amazing story of a woman's journey of ultimate forgiveness and letting go. While Judi Miller's story is specific to her, it holds many lessons for us all. We can all be open to the evolvement of the soul through deep discovery and the willingness to listen to our intuition that delivers us signs all the time. Judi bravely listened and acted on her intuition resulting in her healing and ultimate freedom. God Bless Judi for sharing her story and the healing she experienced. She serves as an example for us to explore our own wounds and stories and find forgiveness."

Lisa Garr
Host of *The Aware Show*

"An honest and raw account of a woman's journey into forgiveness through self-empowerment. Judi's relatable treatise inspires anyone who is ready for true transformation and is willing to move from shadow into light. Spoiler alert: Truth wins out …."

John Newton
Ancestral Clearing & Founder of Health Beyond Belief

"Perfect is a must read for anyone struggling to fit in and who is plagued by fear. This book illustrates the importance of facing our fears, trusting in the uncertainty of life, while surrendering to our intuition to heal. In *Perfect*, Judi Miller courageously shares her story of how she miraculously healed a trauma that was passed down through her lineage. This book is a reminder that miracles can and do happen when we are willing to forgive and love all that is. *Perfect* beautifully portrays how love and forgiveness are the essential ingredients to heal and thrive in life!"

Jennifer Kauffman
Best-selling author of *Shattered*
Executive Producer of Emmy award-winning documentary,
A New Leash on Life: The K9s for Warriors Story

"This beautiful book will open your heart and mind, leaving you full of wonder, hope, and possibility. A who's who among the top energetic and spiritual leaders of our time, this story teaches us that deep and lasting forgiveness is truly possible no matter the circumstance. Thank you, Judi Miller, for your bravery and willingness to write and share this deeply enlightening story."

Kasey Mathews
Award winning author of *Preemie* and
A Mom's Guide to Creating a Magical Life

"This is one woman's incredible journey of healing and transformation. Judi Miller seamlessly weaves some of life's greatest truths into this compelling story of ultimate forgiveness. She provides readers with the tools and inspiration to embark on their own adventure of self-discovery where greater fulfillment, happiness, and joy are in store. This is essential reading for those who want to learn to let go and experience greater peace in their lives."

Suzanne Lawlor
Master Coach, Your Year of Miracles

PERFECT

PERFECT

A Path to Love, Forgiveness,
and Transformation

Judi Miller

www.judimiller.net

Editing: Chandika Devi
Proofreading: Nina Shoroplova
Cover Design: Pagatana Design Service
Book Interior and e-book Design: Amit Dey
Production & Publishing Consultant: Geoff Affleck

ISBN: 978-1-7348350-0-7 (Hardback)
ISBN: 978-1-7348350-1-4 (Paperback)
ISBN: 978-1-7348350-2-1 (e-book)

OCC019000 BODY, MIND & SPIRIT / Inspiration & Personal Growth
SEL021000 SELF-HELP / Motivational & Inspirational
BIO026000 BIOGRAPHY & AUTOBIOGRAPHY / Personal Memoirs

To my mom with all my love

Contents

Foreword xiii

Author's Note xvii

Prologue 1

Part One 7

Chapter One: Being Different. 9

Chapter Two: Miracle After Miracle 21

Chapter Three: The Click 33

Chapter Four: Surrender 43

Part One Integration 57

Part Two **69**

Chapter Five: Finding Purpose 71

Chapter Six: Alone 83

Chapter Seven: The Truth 93

Chapter Eight: The Revelation 107

Part Two Integration 121

Part Three **131**

Chapter Nine: The Risk. 133

Chapter Ten: My Mother's Story 143

Chapter Eleven: Forever Changed 155

Part Three Integration 167

Epilogue 175

Additional Resources. 179

Acknowledgements 181

About Judi Miller 183

Foreword

Albert Einstein once said, "The most important decision we can make is whether we believe we live in a friendly universe." Through my years of work in the field of happiness, I've found that people who are deeply happy always answer yes to having made that decision—even when life is challenging. They believe that they live in a benevolent universe that is supporting their highest good. Judi Miller is one of those people.

Judi's perspective on life is that everything is happening exactly as it should be and that each experience we have is a lesson and opportunity to grow in joy and authentic expression. As she often says, "Everything is unfolding perfectly—we can truly never get it wrong." What a wonderful way to interpret and experience life!

But you may be thinking to yourself, "What happens when things seemingly go wrong? What happens when we feel hurt or betrayed or we don't feel loveable, important, or good enough?" These are completely valid questions. As we are creatures of habit, our habitual negative thoughts and feelings often become the stories we play over and over hundreds of times in our minds until they become our reality.

According to cultural anthropologist Angeles Arrien, in some indigenous cultures, people are encouraged to tell their story when they've had a painful or traumatic experience—but no more than three times. These cultures recognize that it's important to share the difficult story with loving and supportive people in order to release the pain, but repeating it more than three times while hanging onto the pain keeps them trapped in the energy of victimhood. In fact, if a person continues to repeat their story, they'll be dangled over a cliff until they speak only about the wisdom learned from that experience rather than the pain.

In *Perfect*, Judi presents a much easier (and much less scary!) process for freeing ourselves from cycles of negativity. Within the pages of this book, you'll hear her own transformational journey and learn powerful tools to overcome your limiting stories (no cliff involved). The profound and inspiring processes she offers show us how we can transmute fear into love and joy through the power of forgiveness.

One of the greatest discoveries I learned when I was doing research for my book *Happy for No Reason* is that we each have a "happiness set-point." Our set-point, which is based on our genetic tendencies (50 percent), our circumstances (10 percent), and our habits (40 percent) is like a thermostat setting we hover around, unless we do something consciously to change it. Fortunately, we can change our set-point through changing our habits. How freeing! Rather than being victims of our circumstances, we have the power to significantly influence our level of happiness by changing our habits of thoughts, feelings, and actions!

Perfect helps show you how to do that. It invites you to look at life differently and experience greater joy and expansion by shifting your conscious awareness.

I've had the pleasure of mentoring Judi for a number of years and over this time, I've witnessed a dramatic shift in her own happiness level. She's become deeply centered, joyful, and at peace as she's mastered and embodied the principles she offers in her book. Judi is a beautiful, loving soul and a passionate seeker of truth. Her authenticity, warmth, and wisdom radiate throughout the pages of this book. What a gift that she followed her heart in sharing her lessons learned with us.

Perfect is a must read for anyone who wants to experience a quantum leap in their joy. May the wisdom in this book help you experience greater happiness, and may you enjoy the journey with an open and receptive heart.

Wishing you much love,

Marci Shimoff
#1 *New York Times* bestselling author,
Happy for No Reason and
Chicken Soup for the Woman's Soul

Author's Note

This book describes characters and situations from my life and represents my experience of events. For the sake of narrative flow and to the best of my ability, I've recreated dialogue and consolidated certain events in ways that honor their deepest essence. I've changed names and other identifying details in order to respect others' privacy.

I've used the terms *God*, *Creator* and *the Universe* interchangeably throughout this narrative.

Prologue

Have you ever been afraid, plagued by fears that you don't understand? Have you ever felt abandoned and alone? Have you ever had to forgive and let go? If you are like me, you've probably experienced several, if not all of these over the course of your own life. My story may be uncommon, even unusual in many respects. However, the lessons I learned along the journey hold a promise for us all. "What if?" What if that simple question could open up a whole new understanding and possibly change your life?

This is my account of how I transformed. It's a rebirth of sorts; it's a reawakening. It tells of how I went from an accounting professional living a happy, but relatively common life, into a much less common life of acceptance and understanding through awakening my latent spiritual gifts. It's about the process of opening my heart, which took me from feeling incomplete to feeling whole, from feeling solitary to knowing that we are never alone. And ultimately, it's how I learned about forgiveness.

My hope for you is that by following my journey, you will come to a better understanding of how forgiveness works and how you can apply it in your own life. May you learn how to access your heart and let go of your stories, enjoying the process of discovery every step of the way.

The following pages will explain how I got to where I am now, and why I had to walk as I did, detailing my journey from fear, through comprehension, to the absolute understanding of the utter perfection of all things. These pages show how I learned to truly feel with my whole heart, fully embodied, and accept the guidance that was offered to me. It's my hope that they will inspire you to do the same. Doing so brings a peace that goes beyond words. On the outside, I don't look that different, but on the inside I'm an entirely new being—or, perhaps—I'm the being I always was, now revealed.

This book explains how I came to realize that everything, and I do mean *everything*, is perfect.

As I pulled the car door shut, I felt a nervous apprehension move through my body. I was on my way to my healer's house. It was a drive I had taken many times, but today was different. I knew what I was about to do was unlike anything I had ever done before. It was a culmination of the last year of my life; I felt as though every moment of that year, and perhaps of this life and other lifetimes before it, had brought me to this moment.

I started the car and, as if prompted, my phone began to play through the speakers. It was a familiar electronic melody, the same one that had been coming on automatically for weeks. *I need to separate my music account from my kids'*, I thought for the fifth or sixth time in as many days; "Afraid of the Dark" by MKTO was playing again.

I don't dislike the song, but it felt especially inappropriate for the moment. After all, I was *facing* fears, not giving into them. I was about to tell someone I cared for deeply something that could either bring us closer together or move us further apart. I was about to risk a whole lot in order to say something that made no logical sense, but that my heart knew was true.

I decided to pick a new song, one that better reflected what I was feeling. I also wanted something I could sing along to, since I had been practicing singing to help me open up my voice and speak my truth.

Hitting the pause button on "Afraid of the Dark," I searched for the song I wanted to hear and pressed play.

Ed Sheeran's soft, sweet voice began to come through the speakers as I pulled out of the driveway and onto my street. His song, "Perfect," was one I listened to often throughout the process I describe in these pages. It's a love song, though this isn't a story about love between two people. Rather, this story is about the perfection of the Creator's love, which reflects the perfection that we are.

By the time I got onto the highway, I was singing my heart out.

Throughout the drive, I thought about how I had changed over the preceding twelve months. And today as I write this, I reflect on how I've changed in the months since. I am not the person I was when I began this journey. At its beginning, I was racked by fear and uncertainty. I had no idea who I was, really. I felt totally alone in my search. And though I'm still on the journey to discovering who I am, I'm much further along now, and I know I'm not alone; I'm guided by something bigger and greater than myself. I've hit a point where I feel perfect, as Ed Sheeran describes it—except, unlike him, I feel like I *do* deserve that perfection. It's my birthright. I was born perfect, just like everyone else, and we're all still perfect now, despite—or perhaps because of—our perceived flaws and mistakes.

Actually, everything about the story I'm about to tell is perfect. Ed is singing about something that spiritual teachers have known for a long time: The entire Universe is a complicated, interconnected web of events and energies, all of it perfectly designed. It's like a jigsaw puzzle; there may be uneven edges, missing pieces, or even holes in the picture here and there, but as those final pieces snap into place, the perfection of the whole becomes obvious.

This philosophy runs through many cultures. For example, there's an old Taoist fable that tells of a farmer whose horse runs away. The farmer's neighbors share how sorry they are at his misfortune, but he refuses to label it as such; he just shrugs and says, "Maybe." The next day, the horse returns with a herd of wild horses for him to tame and train. The man's neighbors return to celebrate his good fortune, but again, he refuses to label it as such, shrugging once again and saying, "Maybe." Then, when the man's son is training one of the wild horses, he falls, breaking his leg. Once again, the neighbors think this is a deeply unfortunate thing, and once again, the man shrugs and says, "Maybe." Shortly thereafter, the army comes to enlist all the eligible young men, and the man's son is spared due to his injury. The neighbors praise the man's good luck again, but again, his response is the same. The fable goes on like this, with the man alternating between so-called "good" events and "bad" events, but he remains unfazed by all of it. He knows that the events aren't actually good or bad; it's only our stories about the events that make them appear so. And with this understanding, he weathers everything that happens without much struggle.

In my view, the farmer sees everything as perfect—as ordained by something higher, every detail exactly as it needs to be. This is how I see what I experienced, too.

I pulled off the highway and into my healer's neighborhood. The drive was so familiar at that point that it was almost automatic. I passed the large houses and manicured lawns, making each turn without looking at the map; after all, I knew where I was going. In my own journey, I don't always know where I'm going, but I do trust that I will get where I'm meant to be. I trust that each turn has its purpose as long as I keep moving forward with confidence and faith.

"Perfect" was playing for the second time, and I was still singing. I wanted to be able to speak my whole truth when I saw Diana. I wanted to approach her as someone other than the Judi who had come to her months before, preparing for an invasive surgery and dealing with anxiety. That Judi knew nothing about past lives or auras or ancestral healing. She had no idea that trauma can pass down through the generations, and what we choose to face in the present can actually heal the past. That Judi certainly had no clue that what she was entering wasn't just a healing session, but a healing journey—one that would last for the rest of her life.

I put on my turn signal and made the final bend onto Diana's street just as the song was ending. All along the street, the trees were in bloom, flourishing in the spring sunlight. I sang the final notes more quietly, feeling them vibrate through my whole body. I could now see the house and imagine Diana in it, doing whatever she does before I come to see her—perhaps meditating, clearing her energy, preparing to do her perfect work with little Spencer at her side. I wondered if she somehow sensed that today would change everything for me, and perhaps for her, too. I wondered whether she knew that the forces that had brought us together in this lifetime were about to reveal themselves.

Slowly, I got out of my car and walked toward Diana's front door.

Part One

"Life is meant to be experienced in our bodies as feelings without labels, rather than through the stories created in the mind."

— Judi Miller

Chapter One

Being Different

My childhood was fairly typical, though there were always signs that I was different from the others. I was born in Trinidad, the youngest of three children to parents of mixed racial and cultural descent. My father was of Chinese and Guyanese heritage and was born in Trinidad. His own parents were not very present in his childhood, his mother having died when he was young and his father having abandoned him for a new wife and family. He was sent to China to live with relatives, and though they were good to him, his relationship with his family of origin affected his worldview deeply. He could never forgive his own father for abandoning him. As a result, he was never able to teach me how to forgive. I would have to learn the process of forgiveness on my own.

My father tried very hard to connect with his own family of origin, repeatedly reaching out to his one full and seven half-siblings and even going so far as to name me after his stepmother. But these attempts went unheeded; he never found the type of relationship he was looking for there, so he decided to create it with us. He was determined to make sure we knew we were loved, telling us often and showing us by providing us music lessons, day trips to the beach, and annual family vacations. I remember him doing little things like taking us out for ice cream. We could all feel his desire to be the kind of father he always wished he'd had.

We moved to the United States when I was four, and throughout my childhood, we moved several more times. We were not wealthy, but we had everything we needed. My parents were both accountants and did everything they could to support our family.

Like my father, my mother also came from a large family. She was the fourth of eight children. Though my mother's ancestors were in Trinidad for a bit longer than my father's, I actually know very little about her heritage, except that some of her roots extend to China. I believe that our spotty knowledge about my mother's family history is due in part to the amount of pain traveling up that side of the family line. Her father left when she was young, leaving her mother to care for the eight children alone. Her two oldest siblings, Aunt Maggy and Uncle Alfred, became like substitute parents in their father's absence. My mother was a shy child who only rarely spoke up for herself. Her older siblings often had to protect her since she was so quiet. Later, she would go on to become very protective of me, including protecting me from some of the hardest truths of her own childhood.

My mother loved us fiercely, though she didn't speak the words, "I love you," until the day of my wedding. This didn't seem to matter, because I always felt her love. As a talented cook, she often channeled her love through food, cooking our favorite dishes to show she cared. She also made a point to be present—something she still does today. When I was a teenager, she would walk across the street to get me from my late shift at the local grocery store. And now, she comes to stay with me when my husband travels, so I won't have to sleep in the house and face my fears alone.

As a young child growing up in Trinidad, I was often left in the care of Sister Teresa, a nun who liked to call me her child. She truly loved me and felt like family; in fact, if we weren't of different races, I could almost believe we were biologically related. Sister Teresa was deeply spiritual and dedicated to her prayer. To this day, I feel her loving protection watching over me.

My parents were kind but strict. Both my brother and sister, who were six and seven years older than me, respectively, were often punished with a belt. My father said that I was too fragile for corporal discipline, so I either had to do menial tasks, like write what I had done wrong over and over again, or I simply got the silent treatment. To me, this was worse. My father could remain silent for days. He was traditional in that way; respecting elders is paramount in the East, and though he moved us to the West, he raised us with the same values that he had learned as a child.

Those values included a more open understanding of spirituality that is typical of Christian converts from Eastern cultural backgrounds. Both of my older siblings were sent to Catholic school and my parents made sure we went to church regularly. Despite holding a strict adherence to Catholic values and tenets, spiritual gifts ran strongly in my family, and these two realities were not at odds. One of my aunts, Christine, frequently talked about the angels who visited her. My grandmother was able to see and communicate with her own mother, even though my great-grandmother had long been dead. These things were not treated as unusual or even surprising; it was generally accepted in my family that spirits are everywhere and that some people have the ability to sense, see, or communicate with them. Through some combination of my family's Chinese and Caribbean heritage, we were able to reconcile our Catholic faith with a deeper spiritual understanding, even after we moved to the United States. It was understood that up and down our line, some people had heightened abilities. Some people, my family knew, were different.

I am one such person. As a child, I often saw spirits and different energies. I could sense things that came with no easy or logical explanations. I could feel the presence of someone or something and see the movement of energy. My parents treated this as if it were no big deal. They didn't think it was unique or extraordinary. But it scared me. Over time,

I learned to suppress many of these gifts, and by the time I reached adulthood, I wasn't sensing much at all. My gifts wouldn't emerge again for another thirty years.

But some differences were harder to hide. When I was born, I was delivered by a midwife and wrapped tightly in swaddling cloth. It wasn't until later in the day that my brother went to examine me and noticed I had eleven fingers. An extra thumb, connected to the other at the thumb joint, was on my right hand. Half of the extra thumb was removed in infancy; the rest wouldn't be removed until I was thirteen years old, when it was determined that my hand had finished growing and the surgery would not affect my hand's ability to function.

Surprisingly, the kids at school didn't make fun of me for this. Instead, I suffered far more mockery for my race. There were few other Asian children in my classes, and certainly no other Trinidadians. Like my hand, my face betrayed my difference in a way that everyone could see. Just by looking different, I automatically stood out.

This book is not about race or discrimination, but these experiences were formative because they taught me, at a tender age, that being different often means being vulnerable to attack. It's common for people to push away what they don't understand. The threat of being hurt for being different always hung over me. I always had a lot of friends, so I had people to defend and protect me, but it was still disconcerting to know that people were saying and doing things to hurt me without even knowing who I was or what I had to offer to the world. I never asked to be different. In fact, I wanted less attention; I wanted to fit in. But I could never pass myself off as being the same as everyone else. It took me many years to realize this was a blessing. My family background is so mixed that no one considers me "one of them"; Trinidadians don't consider me to be Trinidadian, Chinese people don't consider me to be Chinese, Indians don't consider me to be Indian because I am Indian Guyanese. No matter where I went, I was the only one like me.

This prompted some loneliness, and I spent a lot of my life feeling as though I was nothing. But in that nothingness, I learned I could be anything I wanted.

As a child, I had not yet arrived at this understanding. And somewhere, between suppressing my spiritual gifts and being treated as less than, because of my race, I started to internalize this difference. I was occasionally bullied, and I sometimes had to fight the other kids at school—even the boys. I remember one boy picking a fight with me. The other kids circled around as we began to hit each other. I looked up and was shocked to recognize my brother among the spectators. I wanted him to protect me, to break up the fight, to jump in, or to do *something*, but instead, he just stood on the sidelines, watching. He called out instructions, like, "Hit him in the nose!", but he didn't enter the circle to help me. He stood there, watching me lose. Later, when I asked why he didn't help, he told me he wanted me to learn to defend myself. It would take me years to learn to defend myself but at the time, I just wanted him to protect me.

The experience of being beaten up at school was not the last time I would feel different—prejudiced comments and verbal attacks continued into my young adulthood. I was in college the first time I fell in love. It was beautiful and sweet, like many young loves are. My boyfriend was from a large and totally Irish family and I was good friends with a couple of his sisters. One of these sisters was getting married, and he invited me to be his date. I agreed, and a few days before the wedding, I went to meet his parents. I guess no one—neither he nor his sisters—thought to tell them I was Asian, because they just accepted me as I was. However, when I walked in the door, his parents immediately became upset. They insisted that if I went to the wedding, his father wouldn't walk his sister down the aisle. I was devastated that my appearance had caused such a stir, and of course I didn't go to the wedding; I would never want to hurt anyone in that way. Afterward, my boyfriend tried to keep the relationship going. He even went so far as to move out of his parents' house for a while, because they said that if he kept dating me, he couldn't live with them. He slept on friends' couches, defying his father, but he had no money. After a few weeks, he broke up with me. We were in love and it was the first time I really understood what it is to have your heart broken.

When I met my husband, his family seemed more accepting. We met through work and the relationship progressed quickly. Though he's Jewish and I'm Catholic, we thought we could make it work. I met his parents, Paul and Miriam, and they were kind to me; it seemed as though they were thrilled about our engagement. A month before the wedding, Paul passed away suddenly. It was a tumultuous time in their family. Yet gathering for something as joyous as a wedding still felt right, so we went through with our plans. But then, at the rehearsal dinner, an inebriated member of my soon-to-be husband's family spat out the truth: My husband's parents were concerned about the marriage, Miriam because I am Asian and Paul because I am Catholic. Being deceased, Paul never got a chance to respond to the drunk relative's statement, and Miriam was in such a delicate space that I opted not to bring it up. But I believed that they didn't love or accept me.

We got married anyway, but I continued to struggle with my husband's family for a long time. I never felt as though I was a part of it. I started to label myself as different and always had this sense that I had to prove myself in order to belong. It helped when our son was born; he was Miriam's first grandchild, and she was thrilled. But there were still signs that I just didn't fit into my husband's world. One night when we were out for dinner, one of his closest friends remarked that I wasn't "really" Asian because I didn't have "greasy hair and glasses." His wife kicked him under the table and smiled apologetically, but it affected me deeply, even so far as to make me doubt who I was as a person. These sorts of comments got to the core of my being, making me question the value I had to bring to the world. I was so disappointed to hear that he thought of me this way that I refused to spend time with him again for nearly a decade.

I think the most painful part is when people judge what they don't really know.

That night at the restaurant, I said nothing to my husband's friend. But I've often thought back to that moment. Instead of ignoring the comment, what if I had spoken up? What if I had asked him to get to know me so that he could understand the many ways in which he and I are the same? I also never took my children to visit my husband's relative, the one who said such hurtful things right before our wedding. I didn't want my children to be exposed to that level of prejudice or feel as unwelcome as I did in the family. It took me years to realize that this was my participation in the division; instead of letting him get to know me, I just removed myself and my children from the situation. In doing so, I denied my children the opportunity to get to know their cousins, and I denied my husband's relative an opportunity to know that we are all really the same.

I was different for other reasons, too. As a child, I not only had the ability to feel spirits and energies but I also had a deep set of seemingly inexplicable fears. Everyone has fears; some are easier to see than others, like the fear of public speaking or the fear of spiders, while others are more deeply seated, like the fear of being abandoned or the fear of death.

Some of my fears were obvious—for instance, I was terrified of drowning and was deeply afraid of the dark. But my strongest fear, the one that gripped me in those moments of darkness, was one I kept secret: I was petrified by the idea of being sexually assaulted. Even before I was old enough to really know what sex was, I was convinced that this terrible thing would happen to me.

Night after night, I would lie awake, gripped by the fear of being violated. I never told my parents about this. Somehow, I knew that the fear was irrational; I had never been sexually assaulted. Yet it overwhelmed me. Horrifying scenes would play out in my mind as I lay there in the dark.

This fear continued well into adulthood. Though the details diminished over time, I still kept the light on. In fact, I still often sleep with the door cracked so that I'm not entirely in the dark. A lot can happen in the absence of light.

Though my fear of sexual assault revolved around living, breathing humans, the spiritual aspects of the dark scared me, too. The spirits I felt around me were confusing. I wasn't sure why they were there. Would they help me or harm me? At night, I would close my eyes and beg them to go away, praying to God to protect me. I pleaded to be left alone.

One time, on our annual vacation to Cape Cod when I was twelve, my parents rented a house near a cemetery. I had a friend visiting and in the safety of daylight, we talked about ghosts and demons—but at night, it was a very different story. Later, when we were lying in bed, we heard footsteps. Everyone else was asleep, including my older sister, who was in the same room with us. We tried to shake her awake as the floorboards continued to creak, but we could not rouse her. Then, to our horror, the rocking chair beside us began to rock. My friend and I bolted out of the room and down the hallway to where my parents were sleeping.

Incidents as strong as this one were rare, but the fear of them happening was omnipresent. Every night, I would feel spirits surrounding me. There was a subtle presence that was hard to explain to others. It was as if someone were standing behind me or as if there were eyes staring at me from across the room. I occasionally would see movement in my peripheral vision, only to find no one there when I turned to look. Sometimes, I could even hear their subtle whispers.

I knew that these were the spiritual gifts that ran in my family. At the same time, mine seemed much darker and more foreboding than things someone might consider a gift; these weren't the angels of Aunt Christine's visions, and they certainly didn't provide spiritual guidance. They felt oddly threatening, as if they wished me a harm that they never actually enacted.

It seemed like irrational fear ran in my family, too. Aunt Maggy was particularly tormented by it. I remember how, when we went to visit her, she would check behind the curtains, under the couch, beneath the bed, and inside the closets for intruders before we went to sleep. Given the fears I lived with, I thought these actions were reasonable, but since my mother saw them as paranoid, I kept quiet. I began to watch everyone around me carefully, becoming a silent observer. I learned to walk slowly and with trepidation, for wherever I went, an attacker could be lying in wait.

Over time, I came to believe that living this way was normal. I now see it as something much deeper. And along with this pattern of struggling with fear, I developed another pattern, one that was just as destructive. I began to push down my spiritual gifts. Afraid of what I might sense if I let myself, and afraid of how I might be perceived if I became known as someone who was spiritually gifted, I opted instead to deny this essential part of my being. Instead, I shoved it deep down inside my subconscious.

It would take many years for me to find it again.

Religion provided me some comfort as I combated my fear. I have always loved all things that revolved around Jesus and God. I often use the word *Creator* in this book, but in church, he is called *God*. And some of the teachings about him confused me. I could not understand how we could be born into sin; it didn't seem to line up with my experience of God or of life. I would go to confession and feel almost ashamed that I had not done anything wrong. The priests would insist that I had, of course, for what person could do no wrong? But the things that I did simply weren't that bad. I had a connection with God and I knew that I was unconditionally loved. The idea that people were inherently wrong just felt strange to me. Why would God have made us that way? Wasn't he all-powerful? It seemed to me that our spiritual connection should be about raising up our vibration, showing and receiving love, and reveling in our inherent goodness. It seemed as though, if God had made us, he would want us to rejoice in the perfection of who we are.

The Catholic approach to things felt somber, too. My mother was Anglican, and though my father rarely went to church, he was Catholic and so were we. My older brother and sister were usually the ones to take me to mass. Our home had pictures of Jesus, crosses, and praying hands, but it was all very positively oriented. My parents gave thanks to God for the things we had. The God they taught me about did not judge us or condemn us.

So though I could see the divine beauty in church and any other holy place of worship, I missed the true embodied feeling of the divine love and forgiveness I kept hearing about. I could think about it, even imagine it, but I had never experienced it.

I was an adult and at church with my family when an event took place that changed my life. Or, I suppose, it's better to say that it *began* to change my life. It was the first in a series of mystical occurrences that would forever shape me. It was Good Friday, which to me signifies death and rebirth, and also happens to be one of the rare instances when my husband joins me and our children at mass. He doesn't pray with us, but he sits beside us to support us in our faith. This particular year, we were in a new church, not our usual congregation, so I was interested to see what would happen.

As we waited for mass to start, the choir sang, and suddenly an intense feeling came over me. It was an overwhelming sense of love, magnified a thousand times over and pulsing throughout my whole body. I felt love in all of its forms, such as gratitude, compassion, and forgiveness. I felt all of it. I could barely hold it within me, and it began to overflow in an outpouring of tears.

Over the last eighteen months, I've spent a lot of time thinking about that particular moment. It's often hard for me to find the language to describe what I experienced, and try as I might, I'm unable to really put this into words. The best words I can find still fall short;

even as I work them and rework them, they don't fully capture what happened.

The main thread that weaves together everything I felt that day is "an overpowering sense of love." It came on so strongly that I wondered at the time if anyone else could feel it. Had something just shifted in the whole church? I quickly checked the pews around me, but everyone else was sitting as they had been before, listening to the choir. No one seemed to even notice me. As I marveled at the phenomenal experience I was having, words began to form in my mind, telling me that it was "my turn to step forward and serve." These words were being told to me, but not by a voice; they were being told to me by a deep and profound knowing. I felt these words vibrate throughout my whole body.

I had been touched by the holiness of the Universe. I was in direct and perfect communion with God.

As I reflect on the experience now, it reminds me of the first time I got glasses. I was a child, and it had never occurred to me before that I couldn't see; even when I went to get the glasses, I had no idea what they would really do. Of course, intellectually, I knew they would make me see better, but since I had never had the experience of seeing better, I had no context to help me know what that really meant. I didn't realize that I couldn't see until I experienced seeing with clarity.

That moment was like putting on glasses for the very first time. I had not known how little I was seeing, and then, suddenly, I was aware of a much greater world around me; something richer and more fulfilling than I could ever have imagined before.

I am not normally one to cry. I don't consider myself a very emotional person in general; in fact, I tend to keep things pretty buttoned up. But there in the church, as I felt the love pulsing through me and sank into the truth of what was happening, I burst into tears. These were tears of joy, unlike any I had ever known. And as they streamed down my face, I knew that I would never be the same. Around me, the choir continued to sing, the people prayed and waited, the children squirmed in their seats. From the outside, it looked like everything was just as it had always been. But a sort of reawakening had taken place—a rebirth. I was forever changed.

The Easter story is one of rebirth, and I underwent my own sort of rebirth on Good Friday. But the holiday has a lot to do with forgiveness, as does the story that begins here for me. Jesus's act of forgiveness on the cross was a demonstration of his and God's unconditional love for us all. He loved everyone: Judas, who betrayed him; Pontius Pilate, who handed him over to be crucified; even the Good Thief, who was nailed to the cross beside him. Of the many things Jesus taught, this was his final and most important gift to humanity: *We are unconditionally loved and accepted for who we are; we are never condemned.*

The events of the months to come proved this point eloquently. As I heard the call to my spiritual journey that day in church, I had no idea what I would have to face—or what facing it would bring me. By surrendering to the experience, I was given the knowledge that everything is divinely orchestrated, we are never alone, and we are always loved.

In surrendering, I released my fears and opened to the guidance being offered to me. I also reached back to my ancestors and helped them release some of their deepest family pain, and in doing so, I set all of us free. My ancestors and I were tired of holding all that, and I knew that our destiny—our greatest act of service—is to love.

This is what God does. It's what Jesus did on Good Friday. And I believe this process is an essential piece of reawakening to who we truly are. But to understand forgiveness, we need to be fully human in our bodies—we need to feel. This requires us to release the stories we have created. My journey taught me how this process works and I hope it can be of service to you also.

Chapter Two

Miracle After Miracle

After the shift that occurred on Good Friday, things began to change rapidly. I had undergone an inner experience that was life-changing, but my outer life had not changed at all. I had a great family, a good job, and supportive friends. I was busy and my days were packed. Yet it was the *same* life I had always had, in the *same* part of the world where I had always lived, doing the *same* things. The juxtaposition between this *sameness* and the different way I was seeing the world was almost too much to bear. I remembered the sense of both joy and wonder I had experienced as a child. I wanted to reclaim it. So I asked the Universe for more.

As soon as I did so, the Universe began to answer me. It always does—but it often doesn't answer us in the *way* we expect it to, and this is one such case. Like most of you, I am on dozens of email lists that bombard me with invitations, sales, and promotions all day long. One such email popped into my inbox from an unknown address. I had not signed up for the mailing list—in fact, I had never even heard of the senders! But the two women, Marci Shimoff and Debra Poneman, had created a program that was immediately intriguing. "Your Year of Miracles" promised it would teach me about creating a life where miracles could thrive. I had been interested in self-help for a while, even going so far as to walk across burning coals twice with Tony Robbins in the hopes of overcoming my fears, but this was something entirely different.

The program offered both individual and community support to help me bring my entire life—my relationships, my career, my health, and everything else—into what those associated with the program called the Miracle Zone. It was exactly what I was seeking. I thought I could use the regular reminders to put my development at the forefront of my life, and both the one-on-one sessions and the community surrounding the program attracted me too. I signed up.

I liked Marci and Debra right away. Their program began to reawaken something that had lain dormant for years. I felt a gentle stirring. I wasn't being pushed or prodded, but I was being invited to something greater. It was like a memory of who I was originally, before I tried to fit into society's norms and be who anyone else wanted me to be. I began to see the presence of God in everyone and everything. It wasn't nearly as strong as it was that day in church, but it had the promise of getting there. That promise excited me.

The community connection was amazing, too. Together, we created strong bonds based on shared experiences. These experiences weren't just the things we were doing and learning through the program. I began to see that I wasn't the only one who could see or sense things. There were others with different, incredible, and beautiful gifts to share, like mediums, empaths, and people with subtle vision. Together, we no longer felt we had to hide in the shadows. Suddenly, I was surrounded by a community of supportive women who had some of the same gifts I did—and who didn't think these gifts were crazy or even unusual. Being able to connect soulfully with others and knowing we are not alone in this world are incredibly powerful.

I was also exposed to many speakers who discussed topics I had never heard before. Authors, speakers, and thought leaders like Lisa Nichols, Hans Christian King, and Deirdre Hade expanded my understanding of my life's true path and what I have come here to do. Their talks inspired and intrigued me. I was particularly pulled toward the mystics and psychics whose work felt resonant and important.

Alternative and spiritually based healing drew me in, too. This was an idea that was entirely new to me. I found these speakers to be fascinating. Donna Eden had multiple sclerosis as a child and was able to cure herself. I had never before imagined such a thing was possible. John Newton would get on the phone with someone and within a few minutes, their pain would either diminish or completely go away. At the time, I had no idea what he was doing, but person after person said that it worked.

The same phrases came into my consciousness over and over again. Though these phrases were not new to me, I began to question them in a new way. Things like *open your heart* and *get back into your body* seemed like great ideas, but I didn't fully understand what they meant. I see now that I understood them with my mind but had not experienced them in my body; I had forgotten how to fully feel. I could connect my emotions to thoughts, but not to bodily sensations—at least not most of the time.

I've always been one to embrace things that are new or difficult to explain. I believe that almost everything is possible, even the inexplicable, and I approach most new information with curiosity, simply asking myself, "What if? What if that were true?" These new ideas about healing expanded my understanding of the world significantly.

I had spent much of my childhood asking for my abilities to quiet down. Now I was asking for them to emerge as I navigated entirely new realms of thought.

At the same time that I was being exposed to more and more healing methods, it turned out that I developed symptoms that needed swift and dramatic healing. I had always had relatively light periods, but over a span of about three years, they had become so heavy that they were debilitating. My whole life revolved around my monthly cycle, which was becoming more and more irregular. I never knew exactly when it would occur, but when it did, it was uncontrollable. Moving around made me bleed more, so I had to remain fairly stationary for several days at a time. This made everything difficult, because I never knew when I might suddenly be out of commission. I would work from home, but that wasn't always so easy; I traveled frequently for work, and scheduling trips became very difficult. Traveling for other reasons—vacations, or even to visit my kids in college—also became an issue. I couldn't plan or do anything. I was completely captive to my cycle.

The days I spent at home were scary, too. Though I wasn't in much pain, it felt as though I was bleeding to death. After a while, my doctor told me her greatest fear was that I might hemorrhage and do just that.

I had known Catherine Daniels, MD, for years. As my obstetrician-gynecologist, she had walked me through both of my complicated pregnancies and helped me with nearly every ailment I had suffered. I trusted her implicitly. She was committed to helping me restore my health and get my life back.

We started with a diagnosis. Preliminary tests showed fibroids pushing into the wall of my uterus and causing it to tilt at an unusual angle.

I went for an inpatient procedure to remove the fibroids. It was supposed to be quick and easy. It was anything but. Dr. Daniels was frustrated to find that my fibroids were enormous and pervasive, and she couldn't get near them, let alone take them out. Following the unsuccessful attempt, she strongly suggested a hysterectomy.

I was completely closed to the idea at first. I wanted to get better, but I had to believe there was a better way than cutting into my body and removing an organ. It felt violating and terrifying. I tried to put it out of my mind, focusing instead on the new worlds being shown to me through the Your Year of Miracles program.

Meanwhile, my fear of the dark intensified. I always felt that someone or something was behind me. Each night as soon as darkness fell, I would find myself tiptoeing around the house, paranoid that I would run into someone lurking in the shadows. My husband grew accustomed to me waking up at night and clutching at him in fear, and he began to leave the hall light on. Despite his efforts, I rarely got a good night's sleep, and sleep deprivation began to take a toll on the rest of my life. It was an issue I didn't know how to explain. I had always considered my fear of the dark an irrational fear—I had never been attacked or harmed while sleeping, so what was I afraid of? I had no idea how to even begin to address something so primal and disturbing.

During this time, I scheduled a video chat session with a psychic and mystic. Throughout our session, I felt a large shadow looming over me. The feeling was so intense that I wondered whether it was actually visible in my webcam. The enormous figure was beyond my vision, in a realm that I could feel but not see. It was the first time I had allowed myself to sense such a presence in years, in part because this being felt *far less* foreboding than so many of the others. I was too afraid to turn around or mention it, but I now believe this was a guardian angel watching over me. As the session went on and I explained my increasing fear of the dark, the psychic suggested that I read Barbara Brennan's book, *Light Emerging*. Barbara, a former NASA physicist, spent years studying the human energy field and using what she learned to heal people with her hands. She then spent many years teaching others to do the same through her Barbara Brennan School of Healing.

I purchased the book immediately. When the large book arrived in the familiar, smiley-faced box from Amazon, I was initially disappointed to find that it seemed more like a college textbook than something I would actually choose to read. But then I found myself diving in, fascinated by the stories of people who were healed and who received support from the Universe and their own guides.

The ideas it suggested remained with me, even as my fibroids continued to push torrents of blood from my body, month after month, and as I continued to have trouble sleeping most nights. I didn't know at the time how Barbara Brennan's work would touch me or my journey.

Though energetic healing fascinated me, surgery was really the only option Dr. Daniels suggested. I still hated the idea. And somehow, I felt I had no choice in the matter, which I disliked even more.

At the time, I didn't make the connection to my third thumb, but I later came to realize that I had never had a chance to consent to its removal and as a result my early childhood experiences were carrying over to what I was experiencing as an adult. The first surgery to remove it happened when I was a baby. The second happened when I was much older, but I never got the chance to protest. And on some level, I had wondered what I had done wrong. I thought something must have been inherently wrong with me if the adults I trusted thought my body needed to be altered or "fixed."

I now see that my concern about having my uterus removed was linked to the experience of having my thumb removed. The childhood experience was entirely out of my control, so I felt similarly out of control about my adult situation. My extra thumb had always made me feel sort of special, and the emotional pain I felt from having it removed still lingered in my body. I loved my thumb in my own way. I felt the same love for my uterus. It was an incredible organ that had brought both of my children into the world. The idea of ripping it out of me felt inherently wrong.

Dr. Daniels chose not to push it. She wanted it to be my decision, not hers. She gently reminded me more than once that it was possible that I could hemorrhage to death, and as I continued to bleed uncontrollably month after month her assessment seemed increasingly plausible. Something had to be done. On the one hand, the idea of a hysterectomy felt so wrong. But on the other, it seemed inevitable—as though it was going to have to happen, with or without me. I felt as if it was beyond my control.

I elected to have the surgery about eighteen months after it was first suggested to me. In the physical world, I began to prepare for it. I scheduled the procedure, told my family, and planned time off from work. But in my own inner world, I still had not fully decided. The idea of energetic healing was still echoing within me. If Donna Eden had healed herself from something as devastating as multiple sclerosis, couldn't I be healed from a much simpler condition like uterine fibroids? If Barbara Brennan could heal with her hands and John Newton could remove ancestral patterns in silence, it seemed unimaginable that surgery would actually be necessary.

Amidst these thoughts, I continued to bleed.

The date of the surgery was approaching. I moved forward with my preparations while still not fully believing the procedure would actually take place. It would require me to spend two nights in the hospital and I would not return to work for three months—hard to imagine, given my busy schedule and range of responsibilities, as I traveled frequently and led a large team. The surgery itself would disrupt my life as much as the bleeding did, but then, theoretically at least, it would be over.

My aversion to the surgery manifested as fear. I was *terrified*. I spoke with Dr. Daniels about it frequently. She and I had a great relationship, and I had never had concerns about modern medicine; it had always been a system I trusted. Given all of this, my reaction was uncharacteristic.

I was afraid of the process itself, which I knew would be painful. Dr. Daniels would remove everything but my ovaries, pulling my reproductive organs from my abdomen and sewing it back up again. Without all the organs I had been born with, I worried about being incomplete. But more than that, I was afraid that I wasn't making the right decision. My fears didn't focus around something going wrong or even me dying—in fact, I had always thought it would be fascinating to have a near-death experience—and my thoughts didn't linger too long on the pain itself, but rather, they settled on the idea that it just wasn't right to do something so drastic if it wasn't fully necessary. I found myself scrambling to justify the severity of my symptoms to myself, even though everyone who was close to me, including Dr. Daniels, could see that this was more than an inconvenience.

As I grappled with all this, the idea of spontaneous or energetic healing kept repeating over and over again in my head, finally giving form to the sense of latent anxiety that had begun to pervade my days.

My thoughts were starting to race. I was growing anxious and impatient. One of the guest speakers from Your Year of Miracles, Deirdre Hade, picked me to ask a question in the virtual chat. I asked for help with my fear around the surgery and she had the whole group pray for me. It was quite powerful. I could really feel the energy shifting, and this was my first experience of understanding the potential of group intention. Yet the fear still gripped me.

The week before the procedure was scheduled to take place, I called Dr. Daniels to tell her I had changed my mind. She was on vacation, so I kept getting her answering service. I expected she would call me back right away—she always had—but several messages went unanswered. I knew that though she was out of the office, she was not traveling, so this was quite frustrating. She knew how important this was to me, and she just wouldn't call me back. This increased my feeling that the situation was out of my control. It felt as though I didn't even have the option to cancel, even if I wanted to. I know now that this was irrational, but somehow it felt like the wheels of destiny were spinning and my will had nothing to do with it at all.

As the date approached, I began rather frantically to seek out help from other sources. I scheduled a call with spiritual teacher Sonia Choquette. I had been listening to Sonia for a while but had never before reached out to her personally. I wanted to know if the hysterectomy was the right choice. As we so often are, I was unsure whether the fear I was grappling with was really the voice of my intuition telling me I had made the wrong decision.

Sonia's reading was clear: I would be fine whether I went through with the surgery or not. This was comforting. But part of me wished she would just make the decision for me or point me in one direction or another—which she never did. Instead, she put the question back to me, empowering me to make the decision myself.

I began searching online about healing and energy work. I had never had any sort of energy healing done and I was curious, especially after receiving the group prayer from Deirdre. If I was going to go through with the surgery, I reasoned, I may as well get some support for the fear I still felt around doing so. I was still thinking about *Light Emerging*, and one day about a week before the surgery, I found myself looking up healers who had graduated from the Barbara Brennan School of Healing.

As I scrolled through the list of practitioners, a particular name seemed to call to me: Diana. Something about her name attracted me. Scheduling an appointment with her just felt *right*, among a host of things that felt wrong.

So I sent her an email, typing the words I would come to type many more times: "Dear Diana ..."

Over the course of the next year, Diana and I would send each other dozens of emails. Many of them touched on deep, soulful topics that I had been yearning to discuss with a kindred spirit. But these early emails were much simpler. Diana invited me to her house to receive a healing, which we scheduled right away. With my surgery just a week out, I wanted to have as many sessions as I could fit in before going to the hospital. In those first emails, I asked many questions, revealing just how little I actually knew about alternative healing. I asked her what sort of clothing I should wear, how I should prepare myself, and what would happen. I had never had a hands-on healing before.

Diana answered all of my questions with patience and kindness. She explained that Brennan Healing Science clears and charges the energy field, working with my body's natural healing capacity. Since emotional work often accompanies this type of healing, I knew that there would be some talking, too, and that she would be asking about external factors such as my family, childhood, beliefs, dreams, and lifestyle habits.

Though I still thought energy healing *could potentially* heal my fibroids, I didn't expect the sessions with Diana to do so immediately—the surgery was just a week away. Overall, my goals were more straightforward. I wanted the surgery to go well, and I knew that its best chance for doing so was if I could show up relaxed and ready. A part of me knew that if I showed up at the hospital with all my fear and anxiety, the surgery had a lower chance of being successful and I was likely to face a longer recovery time. Since we are powerful attractors, the vibrational frequency of our thoughts attracts other things that are on the same frequency. What we expect manifests and is reflected back to us because like attracts like. One of our greatest gifts is the power of our attention, and I didn't want mine to be focused on fear. I knew that if I could go into the surgery emanating positive vibrations, that same positivity would come back to me.

The goal of working with Diana, therefore, was to heal my fear and allow me to feel calm about having my uterus removed. If it worked, our sessions together would augment the surgery and help everything go smoothly. But beyond that, I quite simply felt drawn toward her; just as the hysterectomy felt like part of my destiny, she did, too.

By scheduling an appointment with Diana, I knew that I was crossing yet another threshold into a new world. This new world included people who leaned *into* their spiritual gifts, instead of avoiding them or pushing them away as I had always done. I was beginning to shift my perspective on life. I no longer fully believed that things were exactly as I saw them in the physical world.

In some ways, this brought me back to my roots, both Trinidadian and Chinese. The echoes of my ancestors were calling to me. I knew I had spiritual gifts, like many people in my family. I had always had them. I had just never considered them to be much of a blessing. By entering the realm of the spiritual and surrounding myself, more and more, with communities of people who believed in things like healers, psychics, and past lives, I began to normalize those early experiences I'd had when I sensed spirits—the very experiences I had tried to suppress and forget.

Up to that point, my interest in personal development had revolved around things like increasing my self-esteem, getting ahead professionally and financially, and being the best I could be in the materialistic, physical world. But something was still missing. My personal goals were no longer aligning with the world where I spent most of my days. Though I had explored issues of emotional well-being that bumped right up against spirituality, I had just begun to touch the issues of God, fate, and my purpose through personal development—issues I had previously left to religion. I still felt deeply connected to my faith, and Catholicism was still an appropriate container for my understanding of most spiritual concepts. But suddenly, I found myself seeking out people and experiences that would bring this faith together with my personal work, such as seeing a practitioner who would use her hands to assess and heal my energy field, even if I still didn't really know what that meant.

It was an exercise in trust. In many ways, I was taking control of what I could—my healing—even though I was entirely beholden to the symptoms and progression of my illness. And yet I had to trust others to help me. As I see it now, it was fully necessary.

This is because in truth, I was facing much more than uterine fibroids. I was up against a crisis of purpose. My fear of the dark, which had grown as far out of my control as my bleeding had in recent months, was no longer just an inconvenience. Like my cycle, it was beginning to control every moment of my life. And behind both sets of symptoms was a pervading sense that I was stuck in life. I didn't know what I was doing or where I was going. I had everything I had ever wanted—a stable family, a commendable career, financial comfort, a nice home—and though I was happy, I still didn't feel that my life was complete.

The experience I had felt on Good Friday repeated in my mind. Without fully knowing why, I began to focus on the bodily experience that I wanted to feel—that wholeness and love I had felt before, which had bypassed my mind completely. How could I get back there? How could I relive that sense of love, of being touched by the holiness of the Universe?

I wanted to serve humanity. I wanted to do what I came here to do. But what was it? Every time I thought I was close to the answer, it would slip from my grasp. The harder I tried, the further whatever I was reaching for would move away from me. Though I had somewhat internalized that like attracts like, I didn't yet understand that the vibration of reaching and wanting actually pushes things further away.

I struggled to reconcile all of these truths as I prepared for my first meeting with Diana, just a handful of days before the surgery would take place. Somehow, even as I drove myself to that first session, I didn't fully accept that in a few short days I would go under full anesthesia and have an organ removed from my body. It just didn't feel real.

Because it was such a pivotal moment for me, I showed up to my meeting with Diana stripped raw and completely vulnerable. Looking back, it seems like this was exactly how it was meant to be. It was only in that state that I could let the spiritual healing and guidance reach me. Diana came into my life just as I was on the precipice of great change—change I had committed to on Good Friday and again when I scheduled my first healing with her. I was ready for something, and she arrived to provide it. I will forever be grateful to Diana for that. Her kind, nurturing support was exactly what I needed.

Chapter Three

The Click

Diana lives several towns off the highway from me. I was somewhat familiar with the area, but as I drove through the tree-lined streets and saw the fall leaves in their full splendor and the pavements lined with vibrant autumn debris, I was reminded of what the neighborhood looks like up close. The large homes felt more intimidating than inviting and I felt less comfortable among them, as if I didn't quite belong. There was a formality to everything.

This formality melted away as I parked in front of the nice and carefully appointed house indicated by my map app, walked up to the door, and rang the doorbell. Diana answered with her little dog beside her. She introduced him as Spencer. His warm personality came through right away—he greeted me with a friendly wag and proceeded to run in circles around me—all ten pounds of him—as I took in the scene.

The foyer was tidy and well-decorated. Diana herself stood in the middle of it, inviting me in. Her bright, piercing eyes met my own immediately.

As I stepped into her home, I saw the door to her office on the left side of the foyer. There was an essential oil diffuser sitting beside it, gently spreading a pleasant mist throughout the space. I passed through the doorway into the office and Diana followed. Inside there was a massage table, a yellow recliner, a desk, and a bookcase. An altar held important items like a Himalayan salt lamp, a cross, and a feather. Several pictures were on the walls, including one of the chakras and auras surrounding a human form.

I sat in the recliner, as she indicated, and she sat across from me. Spencer curled up on his own little bed. Then, as I answered her preliminary questions, she began to stare into my eyes. Her stare was by no means unfriendly; it was memorable, even unusual in my experience, but still very kind. Yet it was unnerving. Given my Asian heritage, maintaining direct eye contact is something I've had to learn to do; the family culture I was raised in didn't encourage it. But this eye contact is necessary in the corporate world. If you don't do it, you're often presumed to be weak, so to get by I learned how to intentionally look at people with unwavering confidence. This wasn't the way Diana was looking at me, yet there was still something about her look that was uncomfortable. As we continued to look at each other, I heard the "click" of a lock and felt its sonic vibration within me; it was as if everything were suddenly coming together or locking into place. I knew without a doubt that our meeting was not by chance.

I looked away, bringing my focus down to Spencer, who peered up at me from his bed. It felt more comfortable, somehow.

Once the gaze was broken, Diana began to speak, telling me how the healing would go. She explained that it would be more or less like a massage, and I suddenly blurted out, "I hate to be touched!" This is true—my husband knows this, as do many people who are close to me, as I really dislike it when people unexpectedly squeeze my shoulders or try to give me a friendly massage. I was still quite surprised when my response came spilling out as it did.

Diana was unperturbed by my sudden outburst and just thanked me for telling her. She explained that she would channel universal life energy, sometimes called *chi* or *prana*, into my energetic field with the intention of clearing, charging, and balancing my field. She would also call in her spiritual guides for support and guidance. Her hands were merely a conduit for this work to occur. I felt immediately calmer and at her request, I lay down face up on the table. She put on some music. In the way I always do when I'm afraid, I closed my eyes.

I'm pretty much always cold, but Diana's office was quite warm. When she offered to put a blanket over me, I declined. She started at my feet, taking hold of them and rotating them in a circular motion, which felt grounding. Then she spent the rest of the session working her way, gently and methodically, up the center line of my body to my crown, pausing at each chakra. She spent the most time with her hands on my abdomen. With her hands on my solar plexus, she stood over me, breathing gently, for what felt like a very long time. Then she moved up. I had both hands covering my heart and she had to gently pull them away. It felt like she was almost prying my fingers off my chest. Letting go was hard for me—I wanted to protect myself, just as I had done by closing my eyes. But I allowed her to do her work despite my fear. She kept moving up, chakra by chakra, until she reached my crown.

As she worked, I kept my eyes closed, which made it difficult to know exactly what she was doing. I was relieved to note that this was nothing like a massage. Though she was making contact with my body, the work was much more energetic than physical. I could hear her breathing, which was sometimes strange and unusual, and the rattling of her many bracelets. A soft smell wafted from her—jasmine or lavender, some sort of floral scent I could not fully place. I wondered if it was perfume or hand soap. This smell would return to me many times over the next year, either on my drive to work or when I was alone.

I grew more and more relaxed as I began to sense images in my mind's eye. I saw many people whom I love: my children, family, and friends. A single tear escaped my eyes and trickled down one cheek.

She withdrew her hands from my head, and I knew that the healing was over. After a few minutes, I slowly sat up to meet Diana's eyes again. I was surprised to see a look of concern—I thought the healing had gone well, but perhaps she had seen something incurable in me. I quickly realized that her concern was not about my health, but about my well-being. She seemed to want to know that the work she had done in my energy field had not freaked me out or scared me. I reassured her with my gaze in return and processed what she had just revealed about herself. That she was a gentle and loving soul, deeply empathic, who could feel others' pain and who came to this Earth to heal.

As I drove away from Diana's house that day, I didn't know the significance she would hold for me or for my family's story. I did know that something had clicked into place—that the greater wheels of fate were turning, somewhat out of my control. And I did know that the healing she offered was powerful.

It wouldn't take me long to return.

That night, I played my guitar. Several months before, I had picked up my guitar after twenty-five years of neglect, and I found myself playing most evenings after work. To me, classical guitar is one of the most beautiful sounds in the world and playing it has an immediately calming effect on me.

As I processed the day's healing, I pressed the body of the guitar up against my heart and felt the vibration move through me until my whole body felt the music. I felt my heart begin to open, allowing long-dormant emotions to rise up to the surface. I didn't label them; I just let the sound keep vibrating against my heart, and I allowed myself to feel and release whatever arose.

I went to see Diana again a few days later. I wanted to get in as much healing as I could before the surgery—the one I still had not fully accepted would be happening. Like the first time, I drove through the neighborhood to her house. Like the first time, Spencer greeted me and then ran circles around my feet as the essential oil diffuser puffed mist into the foyer. Like the first time, she looked at me with her same piercing eyes—though this time, she didn't stare. But on this second occurrence, I found myself nearly completely closed. I could barely answer Diana's questions. I sat in the yellow recliner, dumbstruck. I was terrified.

I had made the appointment at the last minute. It was the day before my hysterectomy was going to take place, and the hospital called to make a few requests—among them, to ask if I had a living will or a last will and testament. Though I know this is standard procedure, no one wants to hear questions like that, and the phone call had put me into a panic. In desperation, I begged Diana for a same-day healing session to help me calm down. She agreed, but by the time I showed up, I was unable to explore my fear; instead, it was paralyzing me.

There in Diana's comfortable, yellow recliner, I felt like a small child with my arms crossed, refusing to cooperate. I was frustrated to find myself in that state, but it seemed like there was nothing I could do to stop it. When my kids were young, they would often feel wronged or hurt and be unable to let it go. Instead of talking with them about what was bothering them, I often found it most useful to just distract them by talking to them about something else until the crisis passed. This was precisely what Diana did. She suddenly began to act like a parent, distracting me so I wouldn't be afraid. I realized this and for the second time I noted what a patient and caring person she is.

"Have you ever seen a picture like that before?" she asked, referencing the picture on the wall that I had noticed in our first session. It showed a human body surrounded by several fields. Going up the torso and into the head of the body were seven colored balls of light, each representing one of the seven colors of the rainbow. Since I didn't respond, she went on. "Each of those fields represents a part of the human aura, and the seven balls of light are the *chakras*."

I looked at her quizzically. Then I spoke. "I know the word *chakra*, but I guess…"

"You don't know exactly what it means," she interjected, finishing my sentence with an understanding nod. "*Chakra* means *wheel*. Each of these wheels represents the body's energy centers." She pointed to the second one from the bottom, which falls about two inches below the naval. This chakra is orange. She explained that it is responsible for my sexuality and creativity, and that the fibroids were the physical manifestation of some sort of a blockage within that field.

I was so nervous about the surgery that I really wasn't able to take most of it in. She said something about animal spirits, too, suggesting that people have spirit guides who come in the form of animals. I was intrigued.

Then she asked about the books I had read. This was a question I could answer. I began to recount the many spiritual books I had come across in recent years. I remembered a children's book I used to read to my kids, *The Little Soul and the Sun* by Neale Donald Walsch. Neale, author of the famous *Conversations with God*, had boiled down one of his concepts to make it relatable to children. Essentially, through this story he taught that we are all perfect beings made of light and love. As Neale taught, we cannot know our perfection without experiencing its opposite, for there cannot be light without darkness. We agree to learn specific lessons when we are between lifetimes in order to experience all that we are. But by the time we arrive on Earth, we often forget who we are or what we came to do because we are pretending so hard to be what we are not. The two characters in the book agree to their work together before being born. One, an angel of light, agrees to do something really terrible so that the other can experience the power of forgiveness and unconditional love. I explained this to Diana and as I did, I felt the energy shift.

We then began the healing portion of the session. Once again, Diana started at my feet, moved up the center line of my body, chakra by chakra. Again, she paused at my abdomen, gently pulled my fingers off my heart (though this time, she didn't have to work as hard), and moved up to my crown. I smelled the same floral scent I had noticed in our first session. As she worked, I pictured people I love again, inviting my heart to open through the sensation of love and thereby allowing Diana's work to go deeper. I left the session feeling as calm as I could, though I still couldn't fully accept the events that were scheduled to take place the next day.

I went about preparing for the surgery methodically. It would take place in the local hospital, which was the same one where I had labored and given birth to both my children. Except this time, instead of leaving with a child bundled in my arms, I would leave without an organ. The idea seemed implausible.

I would have to be at the hospital at four in the morning, and there I was, the night before, still grappling with the decision. It continued to feel like the wheels of fate were turning without me—as though I just had to catch up to this decision that had already been made or that was somehow my destiny.

As on many nights, I lay down and listened to a guided meditation. These meditations bring me solace and peace. They are not always easy for me, though. I am often asked to visualize, but I don't think I visualize the way other people do. I don't see things with my eyes. Instead, I *feel* or *sense* them. There is the presence of a thing, a place, or a being, but its form remains in my peripheral vision, unseen. Despite my inability to visualize, clearing my mind has always been a worthy endeavor—especially when I'm so anxious. The thoughts race through my head as if on their own accord, and meditation helps me quiet them.

I settled into the meditation easily. But then an unusual thing happened. As I closed my eyes, the energy inside me changed almost instantaneously. Time stood still—the inner time on the other side of my eyelids. I could still hear the voice speaking through my headphones, but beyond it, there was a subtle quietness within the noise.

Then I heard a rushing sound, like something was moving all around me. It was low in pitch and constant. For a moment, I worried that I had listened to something at too high a volume and that my ears had become damaged. But seconds later, I realized it was the subtle movement of energy.

I had entered another plane of understanding, somehow. And on that plane, my panic about the surgery began to fade. Suddenly, I was the one choosing to go to the hospital; I was the one choosing to heal my body by removing part of it; I was the one who was thanking my uterus for its service and releasing it from its duty. Just like when I first met Diana, things were locking into place. The multiple parts of me—the one that didn't want to have a hysterectomy and the one that needed to undergo surgery—were merging into congruence.

As I settled into this new place that was both familiar and unfamiliar at the same time, I heard the voice guiding the meditation begin to close the session. Then, directly in the middle of my vision, a dark figure began to emerge. It was moving toward me and gaining shape in the process. As it grew closer, I began to pick out details: the stealthy movement, the shine of its black coat, the two piercing eyes.

I remembered what Diana had said about the spirit animals that accompany us and I knew that this was mine.

I looked at the black panther, now large and clear and standing directly in front of me. Our eyes locked and we just stared. As she looked at me, I realized the stare looked familiar. The brilliance of her eyes shone against the black, and she stood there unblinking, almost pulling me in with her gaze.

The vision of my animal guide melted away all the fear I'd had about the surgery. I could not rationalize the shift; on the outside, nothing had changed, but just like the experience on Good Friday, I was once again deeply aware that I was being carried by forces much stronger and more powerful than myself. I knew I was on my path. The details—to have the surgery or not—were out of my hands, surrendered to something greater.

I felt this shift throughout my body. When I feel fear, my heart often races. I feel energy and heat rising in my body and my senses are on full alert. Every sound, every movement can illicit panic or the inability to breathe. When I'm calm, my energy is centered within my body. I usually feel as though I am gently floating, suspended and relaxed. But this time, I didn't feel the sensation of floating; instead, I felt completely still.

Before going to sleep, I searched the internet for the black panther, or puma, and its meaning as a spirit animal. The initial search was shockingly accurate. Deeply connected to the feminine, the panther symbolizes overcoming fear of death and fear of the dark. Part of overcoming these fears involves acceptance. The one who is connected to the panther is able to see and understand darkness in a way that many others cannot. She reclaims the darkness as her dominion.

The black panther is a guardian who accompanies the human spirit through this process. As a mother spirit, she keeps her children safe as they walk into the unknown. She is a deeply empowering figure and having a vision of her suggests the beginning of a new chapter.

The panther's presence also indicates a lot about the gifts and talents of the ones she accompanies. People who see the panther are intuitive and artistic. They are introduced to her at the exact moment that they ignite their own passions and discover their purpose on Earth. Her appearance is a nod to the end of a period of pain and suffering. In the wake of this, latent talents—often, artistic ones—will emerge. I was surprised to read that this pain and suffering is often connected to sexuality. As creativity and sexuality are inherently intertwined in the world of the feminine, my research explained, sexual trauma can be released into artistic offerings.

Finally, I learned that there is a profound connection between the panther herself and the ability to see other worlds. Those who walk with the panther don't only exist here, in this time and on this Earth. Instead, they are gifted with the ability to travel to other realms, including other times and other planes, to experience what others have suffered and to heal it with their ability to embrace the darkness that causes all suffering in the first place. The art that they create as a result helps facilitate that healing.

I could see that I was being initiated. The experience of love I had felt on Good Friday was a calling—one I had answered willingly. Through reaching out to Diana, I had taken the next step on my path. The Universe was recognizing this by showing me the panther, whose stare was reminiscent of Diana's. And the physical surrender that was about to take place the very next morning—the loss of my uterus—was a symbolic offering to that process.

I contemplated all of this deeply, still feeling the incredible sensation of having the fear lifted up and out of my body by my animal spirit. Before I closed the window on my computer's screen, my eye caught one more thing: Just like the crucifixion, the panther is a symbol of death and rebirth.

I was humbled and rather shaken by the immensity of what the appearance of the panther meant. I knew I was here to heal and that my creative gifts were opening. The panther confirmed this message. But embrace the darkness? How? I still didn't understand how I could embrace something I feared so completely.

In just a few hours, I would go into surgery.

Every night before I go to sleep, I pray and this night was no exception. I prayed in gratitude for all that I have been blessed with and asked for protection for all that was to come. As I did so, something released. It was as though the fear just lifted. I went to sleep knowing the surgery would happen, and I surrendered to it.

Chapter Four

Surrender

The next morning was surprisingly unemotional. The drama of my resistance to this surgery had lifted somehow. After my experience with the panther, I was finally on board with the surgery, even though I still felt that the decision had been made in some place that was beyond me. I woke up early, got into the car, and my husband drove me to the hospital.

I had relaxed into what was happening—so much so that I fell asleep in my gown in the pre-op room. This was some sort of feat, because I had already been hooked up to countless tubes and wires, bleeding from the attempts to find a vein that was big enough for the IV. I winced in pain as the orderly poked and prodded until he found the right one. Yet despite this, I drifted off to sleep shortly thereafter, waking up to Dr. Daniels's smiling face. Though I knew she would be the one to perform the surgery, I was surprised by how relieving it was to see her. I trusted her completely; I felt ready for what would happen next.

In the operating room, I was strapped to the table. The bright light above me was blinding. The anesthetic came in through the IV and I was asked to count to ten. But before I got there, I was out cold.

The first thing I heard when I woke up was the sound of my own screaming. I've never felt anything like that pain, before or since—even after giving birth twice. A pair of doctors held me down and reassured me as they administered more painkillers. The pain in my abdomen tore through me, ripping me apart, and then before I knew it, I was unconscious once again.

Unlike my first procedure, this one was completely successful. Dr. Daniels had removed my uterus and fallopian tubes cleanly and easily, leaving only my ovaries behind. It was so odd—a part of my body was suddenly no longer there. Yet it was simple, too. I knew that my symptoms had been debilitating, unmanageable. The surgery was the best solution. This part of me had served its purpose, and I have two beautiful children to show for it; now, it was time to let it go.

The panther had led me into the best possible scenario. Later, I was told by one of the doctors assisting the surgery that my decision was not only timely, it was medically necessary. Once they saw my uterus, they realized how extreme the situation had become. I was correct that it was happening with or without me, and I had chosen to get on board while I could still make the decision myself.

But I didn't know that yet. I spent most of that first day heavily drugged; I don't remember much of what was happening around me. I do remember my husband being there next to me nearly the whole time. He sat there in the chair in my room, supporting me as I spent that first night in the hospital and most of the next day.

It was surprising how quickly the hospital staff deemed me healthy and ushered me out the door. They pushed me to stand up, and as soon as I had taken a few steps, they pronounced me ready to leave. Though everyone I encountered there was kind, I found the speed of my exit unsettling. I had barely been within their walls for thirty-six hours. The pain was unimaginable, and it felt like I was leaving far too soon. Yet they said that if I could walk, I was ready to go, and they plopped me back into a wheelchair and I found myself headed out to the car.

The recovery took several months. At first, I continued to be in a lot of pain and I spent most of the first week in bed drifting in and out of sleep. I refused to take painkillers because I didn't like feeling drugged.

During the healing process at home, I began to hear a gentle whisper in my right ear. This wasn't a voice I knew; she had a slight Irish accent. She knelt beside my bed and told me that everything would be alright. She would stay with me for hours at a time, gently guiding and comforting me. She would disappear for a while and then come back to tell me how to take care of myself—how to sit up in bed or how to swing my legs over to the floor and walk to the bathroom. I was comforted by her presence. As my fear waned, my trust in this sort of guidance increased. I found that I no longer wanted the voices that visited me to be quiet. Instead, I wanted to hear what they had to say. I wanted to accept the gifts they had to offer.

The community I had joined in Your Year of Miracles had bolstered my faith in my spiritual abilities. I was less afraid of them. I found myself responding with my common reaction, "What if?", and applying it to the guides I felt and heard by asking, "What if that voice were here to help me?" As I moved into this curiosity and openness, I released my concern that these sorts of events were "crazy."

I had spent my life being so afraid of being alone, especially at night when the unknown hid in the dark. Yet as I spent my long days in bed, recovering, the words of my Irish guide echoed within me, promising a new future on the other end of this surgery. "You are never alone," she told me, "and never abandoned. You are always loved."

Most of the time, I just sense my guides. The hearing is different than an embodied voice—I don't think that someone is physically in the room with me—but it's far more attached to my ears than any other sense, so I call it *hearing*. I had experienced something similar about six months before the hysterectomy, when I began to play the guitar again. A male voice would subtly drift into my consciousness, make a few suggestions, and drift back out again. I found that with his help, I knew how to do things that I would not otherwise have known how to do. For several months, he had instructed me on how to hold my hands, what to play, and how to find the melody. He helped me to express my feelings through music, showing me how to release the emotions that I had denied for so many years. The sound and the cadence began to reawaken my heart, allowing it to feel again. His instruction was very gentle and loving. But then, once I was fully in the habit, he began to fade away.

Similarly, my Irish nurse accompanied me as I sat quietly with the stabbing pain that was left where my uterus had once been. She promised me that God was with me. "If you knew who stood beside you, you would never be afraid," she whispered. As her guidance proved helpful, I trusted her more and more. I thought of the panther and the feeling I'd had on Good Friday. I thought of my aunt Christine, who we all knew is spiritually gifted. I thought of the many other-worldly experiences of my childhood, the ones I had tried so hard to suppress. Like the male voice that instructed me in classical guitar, after a while, the Irish nurse faded away. A few weeks after the surgery, I began hearing from her less and less until finally her voice grew quiet. I don't know whether either of these guides will ever visit me again.

Of course, after these sorts of experiences, skeptical questions come to the surface; they still do. "What if it's not real?" these voices ask. "What if you're making all of this up?"

These aren't audible voices like the guide who accompanied my surgery; they come from inside me as the voices of my doubt. Throughout this journey, I've sat with them a lot. I observe them closely. They're there, yes. They're not going away. They might get quieter, but they might sometimes get louder, too. There's nothing wrong with that.

Receiving this sort of guidance also highlights the importance of boundaries. There are many different types of spirits, and part of learning to accept their wisdom includes knowing which sort of voices to *not* accept. I became less afraid when I learned the simplicity of this process. My job is to set the boundaries and then to allow the ones who make it through that filter to enter. I clearly set an intention that only the beings of the highest light and love are welcome, and then I trust that the ones who come are here to serve me.

The things my guides have taught me have helped me immensely. Welcoming them has only yielded positive results; I'm better for it. So though I still let the voices of my doubt speak—I find that this is far better than trying to suppress them—I don't give them much credence. They don't do nearly as good a job of propelling me down the spiritual path as my guides do. Not only that, but my Irish nurse was right about a lot of things. Just as my guitar instructor made me a better musician, my nurse helped me properly support my body after surgery. During follow-up appointments, Dr. Daniels would make suggestions—the exact same suggestions my Irish nurse had made days before. I had no way of knowing how to maneuver around a surgery like this one. Her wisdom was verified, again and again.

In retrospect, I believe she had come because my guard was completely down. I was weak and vulnerable; I had no way to block her out. When I'm not able to protest, to demand that the world make sense to my mind, my spiritual gifts are heightened. These days I find that the more I relax and let these things happen, trusting in my intention and my intuition, the more I am surprised by how many guides come to assist me—but of course, I didn't understand that at the time.

Shortly after the surgery, I was led to symbolically let my uterus go. It felt like the right thing to do; it had been a part of me for so long that releasing it energetically felt more important than releasing it physically. I decided that I needed to prepare a ritual to honor my uterus. Because I was saying goodbye, it was somewhat like a funeral, but it was also a celebration for all it had brought me.

My husband had taught me the Jewish ritual of putting a small stone on the headstone of the one you love when you visit them in the graveyard. We had done this for years with his father and I had long come to see small stones as reminders of the ones I love. When my own father died, I began to pick up little stones from the sanctuary where his ashes lay and give them to my kids to carry so that he would always be with them. I dedicated one particular stone to him and began to carry it in my purse. There was no fancy, official way to do this; what I did was pretty simple. Most rituals are far more about the intentions than the actions.

I carved out some time to be quiet and alone. Then, I gathered my materials and embraced the silence around me. I have an angel figurine that sits with a small bowl in front of her. I filled the bowl with water, placed the stone in the water and set an intention from my heart. I had done this for my father several years before with a white stone, and I did the same for my uterus with a blue stone.

I looked at the beautiful blue stone with intention and whispered, "I cherish and honor you. You will be with me always." As I ended the ceremony, I slipped the stone into my purse next to the one that honors my dad. I carry both of them with me everywhere to this day.

Dr. Daniels encouraged me to walk daily, and I did, but I would always return to the safety of my bed quickly afterward. The recovery was excruciating—even a cough or a sneeze would send shooting pain ripping through my abdomen—and walking was so painful that I only felt comfortable walking laps around my house for fear that I might trip and fall on a protruding root if I went out to the sidewalk. I went on my first extended walk at the nearby reservoir with friends and family at my side to keep me safe. Hunched over and shuffling, my walk was at a snail's pace, but I felt myself getting stronger and walking faster each day.

During the long hours in bed, I found myself thinking about Diana from time to time. Though I had only met her twice, I felt like we were connected somehow. Just before the surgery, I had sent her a copy of *The Little Soul and the Sun*, the picture book I had told her about during our second session. I still felt badly about my behavior and inability to communicate during that session. Diana had a strange effect on me. I deeply wanted to open to her, yet sometimes my mouth would not cooperate. I hoped that the book would convey what I could not.

She wrote to thank me and we resumed our email dialogue. When I told her that I wanted to come in for more healing but was in too much pain, she suggested a distance healing. I was mostly just lying in bed anyway, so this option seemed perfect.

The idea of a distance healing seemed to be a good fit, even if I didn't fully understand how it would work. Diana assured me that it *would* work, and I trusted her implicitly. The Universe and our guides have no boundaries of space and time, she reminded me, so "hands-on healing" doesn't necessarily require hands.

We scheduled a time to meet, and she called me just before the session to be sure I was ready. I was lying still on my back with my eyes closed, just as I would have done in her office. At first, my mind wandered through the silence. Anxious thoughts began to run through my head—my whole life was continuing without me, with personal and professional obligations going unmet. Though I had planned the time off, I knew work was literally piling up on my desk at the office. And figuratively, it was piling up throughout my life.

These thoughts were still spinning when I began to feel the sensation of heat rising. And suddenly, the pain began to rip through me. The ache in my abdomen intensified to a searing pain, much like the sharp tearing that came with a sneeze. But I was lying perfectly still. The pain took all my attention. I remembered Diana's instruction to lie still, and somehow, I managed to do so, despite the pain. This lasted for around forty-five minutes. It was everything I could do to just keep breathing. Then I received a text from Diana that the healing was over. She told me I could get up and move around, but my body had other ideas; exhausted, I immediately fell asleep.

Diana was right; the distance healing was very strong. In fact, it was the most intense and painful session I had received from her so far. I was really struck by how right she was about her hands not being necessary. Space and time had nothing to do with what Diana was doing. In fact, I had come to realize that she wasn't even the one doing the healing; she was just facilitating it by holding space for universal energy and our guides to come through and do their work.

Shortly thereafter, I received guidance to share some of my impressions of Diana with her directly. I was nervous to do so; I trusted her and felt strongly pulled toward her energy. Yet there were relatively few people in my life with whom I could share these sorts of ideas. The women from Your Year of Miracles were wonderful, but I interacted with them remotely, through phone calls, video chats, and at our annual retreat. The people I interacted with in my day-to-day life didn't speak openly about energies or guides. Even though I knew Diana was different, there was still some concern that she would reject what I shared. I told her anyway. Since expressing myself verbally was still difficult, I did so in an email. I started it simply: "Dear Diana …"

Then I told her what I felt, that I found her to be caring, deep, and compassionate; that I saw her as an empath, and that her sessions were effective. I explained that a shift in the energy occurred after each session with her, and that, while on the surface I experienced a sadness, underneath it was a deep sense of connection—like the type I experienced when I received divine communication. Sometimes sadness and happiness feel the same to me. They both hold a sort of reverence for the Universe and its perfection. They both come as a wave of emotion. The feeling was like that—a wave of deep respect and holy understanding that transcended "good" and "bad" or "happy" and "sad."

I wrote to Diana about the spiritual visitors I had been receiving and how they had led me to her. I told her about the guardian angel that I felt looming behind me when *Light Emerging* was recommended to me. And I explained that this same sort of guidance—the type that comes from a visitor from beyond, or perhaps deep within—told me that she, Diana, had a beautiful, powerful gift, and that she should trust it. I didn't interpret this guidance, I just passed it on.

After I had written a few paragraphs, I sat looking at the email for a while. I decided it was enough and that I shouldn't go deeper. I needed to know how much I could tell Diana without overwhelming her or causing her to think I was strange. So I ended the email, leaving it at that.

Diana's response was better than I could have imagined. She didn't call me weird or crazy; to the contrary, she embraced everything that I had said and took it a step deeper. She told me that she could see that my fifth chakra—the one that lives in my throat and governs expression—was blocked. She also suggested that my emotional level was undercharged, meaning I was not allowing myself to feel. Gently, she reminded me that these blockages may come from pains we have experienced in the past.

I knew she was right. It had not felt safe to feel emotions, let alone express them, for most of my life.

These blockages, she stressed, had once served me. I wondered if their time was up.

Finally, Diana suggested that the re-emergence of spiritual visitors—which, again, she didn't balk at in any way—indicated that I was entering a new phase of life. That part definitely resonated. Something in me had changed on Good Friday, and now suddenly, everything seemed to be moving quickly.

My healing was progressing and Dr. Daniels gave me permission to drive again. Painfully, I made my way to the car to see Diana. I was trying to move as little as possible; the dull ache was ever present but then I would suddenly feel an electric shock shooting through my abdomen and I would be unable to move or even to breathe.

I walked up to the house, which was now familiar. The gray deciduous trees sported bare branches while the evergreens shone brilliantly in the crisp, cold sun. I rang the bell and greeted Spencer, whom I truly enjoyed seeing each time. He was becoming more and more friendly with me. I spent several minutes just connecting with him before looking up. And there was Diana, once again welcoming me into her home for healing.

She began by checking my chakras with a pendulum, which is a small, pointed weight that dangles from a small chain. I had only seen a pendulum once before, but she explained how it worked. The practitioner grasps the top of the chain and holds it over an energy center and asks a question. Then, as if on its own, the crystal begins to swing. The pattern of that swing—forward and back, left and right, clockwise or counterclockwise in a circle—tells the practitioner how the energy is moving. As Diana held her pendulum over me to diagnose what was going on with my body after the surgery, I found that I trusted her nearly as much as I trusted Dr. Daniels, whom I had known for many years. Though while I trusted Dr. Daniels with my life, I was beginning to trust Diana with my soul. I was anxious to hear what Diana saw, sure that she would be right and that she could help.

She started at my lower chakras, stopping at the second one—the sacral chakra—and explaining that she felt a lot of activity there. This was natural, she stated at first, because I was healing from surgery in that exact area. But she intuited something else, too: Sexuality and its less-sexy counterpart, creativity, could have been creating the blockage that led to the fibroids in the first place. This aligned with what I had read about the people who are connected to a panther animal spirit, but I didn't fully understand it. I knew I would benefit from exploring my creative gifts more, but I didn't think my sexuality was blocked; I had *feared* sexual assault my whole life, but I had not *experienced* it. When she got up to my throat chakra, she repeated what she had said in the email: I needed to express myself more. I knew that this was true. For most of my life, I had noticed that formulating what to say seemed to come more quickly to others than it did for me, and even when I could figure out what to say in time, I struggled to open my mouth and speak the words. But when she swung her pendulum over my third eye, she said something that I wasn't quite expecting. My third eye, Diana remarked, was almost completely shut, in contrast with my crown chakra, which she saw as quite open.

On some level, I knew this. Since embarking on this journey into metaphysical and spiritual concepts, I had heard many people speak about visualizing things as clearly as if they were watching a movie on a theater screen. My version of visualization, on the other hand, is much more subtle. I sense things, but it's rarely with one of my physical five senses. When I close my eyes, I usually only see darkness—more like the theater before the movie begins. Besides this, I had spent a good deal of time as a child trying to repress the images that did come. I told Diana that I was not surprised, yet it was a strong statement, nonetheless. We spent most of the rest of the session in silence.

I began to schedule weekly sessions with Diana. By now I was walking the two-mile loop around the reservoir every day, and though my recovery was still slow and painful, I was relishing the time away from work when I could focus on something that had become far more important than my career: My development as a spiritual being inhabiting a human body. As I progressed in healing both my abdomen and the sacral chakra housed within it, I found myself using my throat chakra more and more to share with Diana. The talking that I had so dreaded when beginning my sessions with her were becoming increasingly comfortable. Some sessions were spent mostly on the healing table. I didn't always have a specific ailment to address so we spent more and more time talking about life. Between sessions, these conversations continued in a series of rich emails. I was beginning to trust Diana enough to open my heart to her.

I knew from reading Barbara Brennan's book that Diana's healing method is based on the theory that many of the blocks in our auras and physical bodies come from our past experiences. There are seven layers of the auric field, and in the center of them, there is a light that emerges from the very center of our humanity. It is through accessing this light that we can heal ourselves. It also helps to take a look at our past with fresh eyes so we can understand what's going on. By doing so, we heal psychologically as we heal physically, which unblocks our auras on two levels at once. Some of these blocks come from our early childhood experiences, and since many of the most impactful ones involve our parents, Diana and I began to discuss my parents more and more.

My mother always had trouble expressing herself. She is a wonderful woman, generous and kind, and she has always wanted the best for me. Telling me how she feels isn't easy, though. Despite her lack of verbal communication in this area, I always felt loved, and she showed her affection through her actions, which always put me ahead of herself.

Similarly, my father showed me that he loved me in a thousand and one ways. I never lacked for love. Yet he struggled with trust and forgiveness. His father's rejection had left a sting that never went away, and his half-siblings didn't embrace him the way he wanted them to. While he could tell me he loved me with his words, I don't know if he could ever tell *them*; I don't think it would have necessarily been well-received, and trust was hard to come by as a result. Forgiveness was out of the question.

I began to connect the blockages in my chakras with these early experiences. Our parents teach us how to walk through the world, for better or for worse, and we interpret what they teach through our own filters. On some level, I interpreted my mother's lesson as *don't speak*, and my father's as *don't forgive and don't trust*. But I put my own spin on things. While I could easily tell those who were close to me that I loved them, I found it harder to speak other truths, blocking my throat chakra. And while I could trust my family to not reject me, I couldn't trust them with *all* of me—particularly the part that housed my spiritual gifts. This made it hard to trust anyone else with the secrets of what I felt and experienced, too, and sometimes hard to trust that the things I sensed were even real at all.

We also discussed my fears, such as my fear of the dark and my fear of drowning—though I still didn't feel safe enough to share my fear of sexual assault. It was much harder to find a psychological root for these fears in my childhood, and after countless sessions, we decided to leave them unexplained.

Diana began to speak to me about past lives, something I had rarely considered and knew little about. She suggested that the unexplainable fears and burdens we experience in this life often have transpersonal roots, meaning they can be traced back to the lifetimes our souls lived before. She introduced me to the work of Brian Weiss, MD, who specializes in past-life regressions. Then she explained that some people reconnect with others whom they had known in another lifetime and she recounted her own experience with this phenomenon. Diana shared that at one past-life regression workshop she had attended, it was revealed that the teacher of the workshop had murdered her in a past life. He was devastated that he had inflicted so much pain on another. I had never heard anything like this before and I was fascinated.

After we talked for a while, I would go to the healing table and Diana would begin the hands-on portion of the session. Like always, she would ground my feet and move up my body, chakra by chakra, until I was clear.

Sometimes we would process what I experienced afterward, but more often than not, we would run out of time and I would share my experiences with her later in an email. These emails began to stimulate my creativity—they required me to trust her enough to share, and then find the right words to make my feelings tangible. They became a part of our work together.

With each healing session, I felt myself opening. At this point I was healing far more than my hysterectomy—I was healing my whole life.

Part One Integration

Reflections

Looking back, I can see that I was in the process of learning the truth about the divine order of the Universe and the perfection of who we are.

To experience that perfection, we need to fully embrace our human experience. That means getting out of our mind and into our body to access our heart. We need to experience life without the stories, labels, and judgments the mind often creates and allow these events and feelings to be fully processed and released through our body.

We're often trained to think about our emotions. But when we think about them, we don't truly embody them; we don't *feel* them. We need to be in our body to access our heart because it is only through our heart that we can experience our divinity—the wholeness of who we are.

Our stories about what was or will be limit our ability to feel in the present moment. These stories—most of them quite negative—are made up of thoughts, and they can create blocks that prevent us from letting these feelings move through us. Much like Diana was removing blocks from my aura as I lay on her table, I was removing blocks around the way I saw the world through the experiences I was having. I was expanding my consciousness and believing that more was possible. This openness dissolved many stories, freeing me up to feel more.

As I did so, I began to understand how these stories drive our lives and prevent us from accessing our hearts. I started to see how life is meant to be experienced in our bodies as feelings without labels, rather than through the stories created in the mind.

These truths are universal. I'm not the first one to toy with them, and I won't be the last, either. In the late eighties, Stephen Covey wrote *The 7 Habits of Highly Effective People*. I had read it at the time, and his wisdom stuck with me through the years. As Stephen wrote, "Between stimulus and response is our greatest power—the freedom to choose." We have a choice. The way I see it, we can truly either embrace the now, feel an experience, and then let it go, or we can choose to create a story that will then live on until we learn to surrender.

We have over 60,000 thoughts a day. Ninety-five percent of them are the same ones we had yesterday and 80 percent are negative. We keep playing the same stories over and over in our minds and somehow expect a different result. These habitual stories can often manifest as pain, sickness, or trauma that lives in our bodies. This pain and these burdens will not leave until we learn to let them go.

Science shows us that truly feeling an emotion is a quick, nearly immediate experience; it usually takes no longer than ninety seconds. Jill Bolte Taylor, PhD, a well-known neuroscientist who was able to heal from severe brain damage, teaches us what this ninety-second barrier means in her book, *My Stroke of Insight*: That once our ninety seconds are up, it's up to us.

As I understand it, everything from that point forward is just a story. "Moment by moment," she writes, "I make the choice to either hook into my neurocircuitry or move back into the present moment, allowing that reaction to melt away into fleeting physiology." Again, she mentions that it's a choice.

As I see it, the choice is between creating a story or not. And here's why this is so important: When we're in a story, we think we're feeling the same thing over and over, but in truth, we're not feeling it at all; we're *thinking* it instead. Because we don't feel or acknowledge the sensations that accompany emotions, we can't release the emotions themselves and they become stuck. Then, in a misguided attempt to understand our emotions with logic, we create stories about what everything means. "He said that, which means he thinks this about me." "I suffered in that way, which means I am like this."

The best way to let a story go is to not create one in the first place. I think I've always been naturally inclined to create fewer stories. I find that when I just let things happen without giving them too much meaning, I don't create so many negative patterns in my life, and I don't end up carrying so much baggage. This makes life much lighter. I process things quickly and just move on.

I believe this can be attributed to my parents. Though I received many gifts from them, two are worth mentioning here. The first was unconditional love. While I felt the world around me was quite judgmental, unable to accept me for who I was, my parents reflected a different way to live. The other gift they gave me was that they were extremely bad storytellers—not in terms of the stories we tell children for entertainment, but in terms of the stories we tell ourselves about the deeper meaning behind the events of our lives. My parents simply didn't do that. Whenever something happened, they went with the flow, much like the farmer from the old Taoist fable I told in the prologue, the one who said, "Maybe." I learned that they just didn't try to control things or define them by putting labels on everything. They instilled this in me; they made me a bad storyteller, too.

But like everyone, I get caught up in my stories sometimes. While you can look back at the previous chapters and find plenty of these stories woven through my experience, I'll identify three of the main ones here.

The first is that I felt I was different. This comes from something that is actually true; I was different and in many cases I was treated that way, whether it be for my race, my nationality, or my cultural identity. Because I was also afraid, I didn't expose myself as having spiritual gifts, but deep down I felt that I was different in that way, too. As I now believe, everyone has spiritual gifts, but not everyone allows themselves to express those gifts. I certainly didn't allow myself to express my own, choosing instead to see myself as being different for having them.

The story I created around being different followed me throughout my life. And it affected many things. In my marriage, for example, I took the things I had heard from my husband's relative to mean I would never be loved or fit into their family. I believed what he said about Miriam's view of me, and I never let her into my heart completely. At work and in social situations, I walked through life feeling that I had to be the best version of myself. I spent massive amounts of energy trying to prove my value to myself and others because, deep down, I believed that I didn't have any.

The second story I will highlight here is that I could not use my voice. At a young age, I got the idea that I could not speak; that even if I did, my voice would not be heard. I found this extremely annoying. I constantly had trouble putting my thoughts together, and when it came to expressing them, I would often find myself frozen. Sometimes someone would even be physically hurting me unintentionally and I would remain silent, unable to admit that I was in pain. Over and over again, I repeated the story that I could not use my voice—and, lo and behold, it appeared to be true.

The third is the idea that I was incomplete. This came to the surface when I began searching for my life purpose after Good Friday, but the story had been with me all along. It may have started with losing my extra thumb, but I'm not exactly sure where or when I first had the thought that I was incomplete. By suppressing my spiritual gifts and not living from my heart, I was denying essential parts of myself, and incompleteness became a wound within me. By the time Dr. Daniels suggested the hysterectomy, the idea of ripping an organ out—making me more incomplete—felt as though I would be destroying something core to my being.

I didn't know how to fully feel emotions as sensations in my body yet, so I just repeated the stories over and over again: I am different. I cannot use my voice. I am incomplete.

And the thoughts that accompanied them were agonizing. They caused me to behave in ways that were ultimately not in my own best interest, and I could see the negative results rippling out through my life, but I didn't know how to stop thinking them. In part, I didn't know how to stop thinking them because by thinking them, I could avoid actually feeling them. And in part, I didn't know how to stop thinking them because I had convinced myself that they were true. I realize now that my mind created this problem, and only my body could offer the solution.

The first step to dissolving our stories is to become aware of them. We have to recognize that we're telling ourselves a story—that in that pause that both Stephen Covey and Dr. Jill Bolte Taylor describe, we have chosen to create something unnecessarily.

At this stage in the game, I was becoming increasingly aware of my own stories. My guides were helping me with this. They were showing me the other side of that choice: the option to just let myself feel. They also showed me that they were there to help me—that we live in a loving and supportive Universe. Honestly, I think that the emotional vulnerability around not knowing my purpose and the physical vulnerability I experienced after the surgery made space for them to enter. I was unable to block them out—something I had been unconsciously doing since I was a child. But in my vulnerability, my heart was open, allowing the highest spirits around me to open it even further. And with their wisdom, I found that I could dare to be different by exposing my spiritual gifts and even encouraging them to develop. I found that I actually could use my voice, at least sometimes, with the women in Your Year of Miracles and with Diana. And I could allow myself to do what was medically necessary—surrender my uterus—even if it threatened to make me even more incomplete than I already felt. I could do all of this while feeling my emotions fully and without labeling them.

This takes courage. It takes inner strength. But it also takes a readiness. Each one of us has our own timing with these things; each one of us begins to wake up when he or she is ready. For me, this is when it began.

Exercises

Everything in life is just energy, vibrating at different frequencies. All that appears solid in this world (the trees, the rocks, a table, and even our bodies) is simply energy, densely clustered and vibrating, which creates the illusion of solidity. Science has even proven that thoughts are things—energy frequencies that can be measured and observed. I found through simple practices, I was able to begin to feel again and direct my energy in ways that supported me.

The simple exercises below will help you do the same.

Move, for You Are Energy

Just like the energy that surrounds us, we are energetic beings. Every fiber and organ of our body is made up of energy. This means that we can change our state of being instantaneously by moving the energy that lies within us. One of the easiest ways to make a shift is by changing the way that we stand, the position in which we hold our shoulders and our head. Everything is either expanding or contracting; our energetic state follows our physical state.

This is a simple exercise I learned many years ago. Watch what happens when you make this simple shift:

1. Stand up straight with your shoulders back, your chin straight ahead, and your eyes looking slightly upwards. Then, smile widely. Note how you feel.

2. Now, hunch your shoulders forward, tuck your chin toward your chest and look down with your eyes. Furrow your brow and frown. Note how you feel.

In the first position, it is easier to feel happier and more confident about life. Your mind and spirit are expansive, matching your body. In the second position, everything feels heavier or sadder. Your mind and spirit contract along with your body. Noticing how this small bodily change effects your entire state of being can be very powerful!

Anytime you want to make a shift, check in with how you are holding your body. Make sure that it is congruent with the energetic state you want to be in.

The laws of physics also teach us that an object in motion tends to stay in motion. Consequently, movement provides our life force with the energy and momentum it needs to heal more quickly, to move forward in our life and manifest that which we seek.

After my hysterectomy, hunched over and shuffling, I walked the two-mile loop around the reservoir every day for seven weeks. Movement allowed my body to heal more quickly by moving the energy within—the walks stimulated blood flow, which was necessary for tissue repair. Movement doesn't just help us physically. Whenever I felt stuck in my life, I realized that my energy was also stuck; I had begun to stagnate. When I began to move again, my energy expanded. With that expansion of energy, I began seeing and experiencing more and more possibilities around me.

Tony Robbins says, "Motion creates emotion." The mere act of moving can change our state and our energy instantly. And the best way to move is in a way that brings us joy so we can look forward to doing it. When we are in a state of joy, everything feels easier. This is enhanced when we commit to the practice with someone else—it can amplify our experience and provide us with a built-in accountability partner.

To give yourself an energetic boost, try the following thirty-day practice:

1. Write down one or two activities that will help you increase the current level of movement in your life. A few examples are walking, dancing, gardening, and cycling. Any physical movement will do, as long as it's right for your body. If you have an illness or injury, be sure to check with your physician about which activities are right for you.

2. Commit to doing the activity (or activities) for at least a few minutes every day for thirty days. You may also want to choose the specific time of day you will commit to doing the activity. I

prefer exercising in the morning as it gets my energy moving for the day ahead. What you decide is up to you; the most important thing is that you follow through on your commitment.

3. Remember to begin gradually and don't be discouraged if you don't see or feel changes immediately. They will build up incrementally over time and can add up to amazing, life-changing results.

4. By committing to the activity for thirty days, you will have created a habit and the feeling will be anchored within your body. You will have created a shift. You will no longer have to consciously think about performing the activity. Your body will naturally crave the feelings created by the movement.

Create, for We Are the Creator

At our core, we are a creative life force. This creative energy must be expressed or it can stagnate and materialize as pain or sickness in our bodies. Consequently, we need to allow this creative energy a form of expression.

There are countless ways to express creative energy. Writing, painting, dancing, singing, and playing an instrument are all examples. Expressing creativity doesn't have to mean making an original work, like writing a song or painting a picture from our imagination. Any activity that asks you to think differently uses creative energy—coloring a mandala and doing a puzzle are great examples of creative expression, too. We get to choose.

For me, writing and playing the guitar are my outlets. When I began to play the guitar again, it provided me with a creative and safe way to feel and express feelings that had remained dormant for many years.

But my creativity was not just limited to those activities. I also found creative expression in the simple acts of life, from the presentations I put together at work, to the food I prepared for my family, to the clothes that I chose to wear.

How do you want to express your creative energy? This simple exercise will help get you started:

1. Identify up to three things that you can do that allow your creativity to flow. You're looking for things that help you express yourself in a new and different way.

2. Incorporate these activities into your weekly routine. Make time to express your creativity at least two or three times a week.

3. Make sure to change it up periodically and do new activities. Because you are a creative life force—you are a creator—your soul thrives on discovering new things.

4. Make creative expression a conscious choice and you will see the creative life force within you begin to move, flow, and manifest.

Disrupt the Stories

We all create stories at some point, and unfortunately, most of these stories are based on our interpretation of events that may not reflect complete or accurate information. Once we've created a story, we play it over and over in our minds until it becomes our reality. However, we can disrupt or let go of these stories once we recognize them and determine that they no longer serve us. Disrupting the stories creates a pause, and in that pause, we get to choose: Do we want to continue that same story, or do something different?

Let's start by observing the pattern of your thoughts. What are your stories? What are the thoughts that you gravitate toward out of habit? Here are some examples of negative stories: *I am not good enough. I am not smart enough. I am not pretty enough. I am not rich enough.* If you believe any of these to be true, you will attract people and events that support this belief.

We are bombarded with billions of bits of information each second. We act like powerful magnets that attract more of whatever we focus on. That's why one of our greatest powers is to choose where we place our attention in any moment. We can do this by asking ourselves, "Where is my attention now? What am I focused on now?"

When we begin to track our attention, we start to notice how often we subconsciously choose negative thoughts over positive ones. We often think that we are not enough, that we are not loved, or that we are alone. But none of this is true! We are the creator of our own life. What is it that you want? Focus on that!

There are moments in life when we forget. We get caught up in an event and we revert to our familiar stories. Our stories are made up of thoughts. Thoughts, like stories, are not always accurate and can be changed. Just like the needle on a record player, we slip back into the groove of a familiar track and suddenly we're playing it repeatedly. If you want a different result, you have to scratch that record until that song can't play anymore!

As Tony Robbins explains in *Awaken the Giant Within*, there is great power in interrupting our own patterns. Let's say your new desire is to greet the day with high, positive energy. But every time you roll out of bed, you immediately start feeling grumpy thanks to the endless to-do list that starts firing in your brain. Rather than sink into that pattern, interrupt it! Start singing your favorite song in a loud happy voice or raise your arms above your head and shake your hands as if you were shaking off all that negative energy. These types of actions will immediately break your pattern, so that you can then replace the negative story with something more empowering.

When we're stuck in an old, negative story, interrupting the pattern to replace it with either a new, more empowering point of view or something positive is a fantastic way to make a change.

Try this exercise:

1. Observe your automatic and learned responses to events and people. Through observation you create the awareness that will enable change.

2. Once you are aware of those negative "grooves," choose a pattern interrupt that will effectively scratch the record when the negative story starts to play.

3. In the space created by scratching the record, you get to choose your next move.

   o You can replay the old, negative story.

   o You can choose to see it from a new, more empowering point of view.

   o You can take it to the body.

These actions will create an awareness around the stories of your life. In that awareness, you can begin to let them go.

Take It to the Body

At this stage in my journey, I was learning to process life as sensations in my body and letting go of old stories that no longer served me.

Now, whenever I have a negative charge around an event, I almost immediately take it to the body. I notice where I feel the sensation in my body. I breathe slowly and deliberately into the affected area. Within seconds, the sensation and charge begin to dissipate. I believe this works because I am breathing the breath of life—my energy source—into the area.

For example, when I think back to the prejudiced comments I heard throughout my life, I ask myself: *Where do I feel it?* I used to feel it as a heaviness that sat on my chest like a giant elephant. I've learned to acknowledge the sensation or feeling by squeezing it back, breathing into it and releasing it.

As a trained facilitator in Dr. Sue Morter's *Energy Codes*, I find central channel breathing extremely effective. The following exercise is adapted from her book, *The Energy Codes*. Before trying it, it's important to understand how to breathe through what Dr. Sue calls the central channel. The central channel runs vertically up and down the center of your body, extending slightly above your head and dropping straight into the earth below the pelvis. Imagining the breath moving up and down this channel as you breathe can help expand your energy.

This is a useful exercise for when you feel a negative story starting to form due to an event that takes place. After an event occurs, do the following practice:

1. Notice where in the body you have a sensation.

2. Squeeze or contract the muscles in that area if you can. If you can't, imagine yourself doing so.

3. Start your central channel breathing, using your mind's eye, inhaling slowly beginning above your head, then down through the center of your brain, the center of your throat, the center of your chest, pulling the breath down into your belly, and then exhaling it through your pelvis and dropping it down into the center of the earth. Then, reverse course by inhaling and pulling the energy up from the center of the earth, into your belly and then exhaling through each of the major points in the center of the chest, throat, and brain before bringing it back out through the top of your head.

4. Along the way, as you pass nearest to the place where the bodily sensation is located, imagine the breath enveloping the sensation and pulling it into the central channel.

5. Perform two complete rounds of breathing up and down the central channel as you feel the sensation begin to dissolve.

Part Two

"The essence of who we are is love. As love, our purpose
is to expand and to create, for we are the Creator.
The reason we are here, alive, is to experience
who we are."

— Judi Miller

Chapter Five

Finding Purpose

Diana leaned forward in her chair. "What do you mean, ask you questions? What kind of questions should I ask you?" she said. As she did, Spencer got up and began turning in circles on his bed, looking for a new comfortable position. I watched him briefly. Over the months that had passed since my surgery, I had come to really appreciate Spencer. I had always liked him, his discomfort somehow seemed to mirror my own.

I had just told Diana she could ask me any questions she wanted, assuming they would be about spirituality or the nature of the Universe—something deep. But now that she had asked the simplest question—now that she had asked me to explain my sudden statement—it was hard to do so.

There was so much happening in my world and few people in my close circles could really understand. Strange experiences, visitations from guides, and sudden *knowings* were frequently interrupting my days; in fact, they had become part of my days. And I was acutely attuned to the fact that the life I was living was no longer serving my purpose. I needed to make a change, but first, I had to figure out what my purpose *was*. It was frustrating. I knew I was being called to do something, but I didn't know what it was. The very idea of my purpose had begun to bother me; it was elusive, something I could never quite catch. *Why was I here? What had the Creator sent me to do?*

I had come to rely on Diana to help me make sense of it all—especially the downloads. I was getting more and more random downloads of information from the Universe. I hoped I could provoke the downloads somehow, calling them into being.

"The information I'm receiving, it often feels channeled," I explained. "It feels like it's not really me saying it. Or maybe it is me—maybe it's part of my higher self, the higher knowing that lives within us all."

Spencer shifted again, moving himself off the bed and over to Diana's feet. I began again, hesitantly. "I guess I don't exactly know *what* it is, but maybe if you ask some questions, more of it will come."

On the outset, I was challenging Diana to come up with questions to ask me. But I knew I was challenging myself, too. Answering questions had always been hard for me. It was often difficult to open up, and even when I fully wanted to, self-expression always felt like something that came easier to other people than it did to me. So often, I could think of the energy of what I wanted to express, but the words just wouldn't come. This seemed particularly strong when I spoke with her. I struggled to grab onto the right word, like I was translating from another language.

Later, as I lay on the table, I told Diana that I was worried my search for purpose had become part of my story—an excuse for not taking action. Diana said she would do a scan of my body, chakra by chakra, to look for blockages. By then, my abdomen hurt only rarely and the pain was centered around the incision itself. She had long passed the point of healing the wounds caused by my surgery and was now working on my energy more generally.

As soon as she laid her hands on me, I heard a strong buzzing sound. Bizarrely, it sounded like a scanning machine one might find in a hospital. As it grew stronger, a horizontal beam of light appeared above me and droplets of light began to rain down on my entire body. With open eyes, I watched the light shower over me. I blinked once and the image was gone, as soon as it had arrived. The sound was gone, too. All I could hear was Spencer's soft breath as he slept soundly.

About thirty minutes later, I said goodbye and began walking out to my car. Diana had just closed the door behind me. I was about halfway down the walkway when she opened the door again. She called out, "What is *our* purpose?"

I turned around. "What, like you and me? Or all of us?"

"All of us," she responded.

I paused and told her I would have to sit with it but promised I would respond. I drove home contemplating the question she had asked me.

Several days went by before I answered her. The question sat with me as I took my slow walks around the reservoir, folded laundry, fed my dog, and ate quiet dinners with my husband.

"Dear Diana," I typed. The cursor blinked in front of me.

I closed my eyes, trying to feel what I had felt on Good Friday.

Then my fingers began typing.

The essence of who we are is love. As love, our purpose is to expand and to create, for we are the Creator. The reason we are here, alive, is to experience who we are.

I took my hands away from the keyboard. I knew that more was needed, but I wasn't sure exactly what.

I thought back to the rest of my life and how I had changed in recent months. I had always suppressed the part of me that was different in an attempt to be accepted. But as I continued to evolve, I was becoming increasingly different from my friends and family. It was scary, but it felt like the right thing to do; to be fully myself, I had to let myself be different.

I had to remember who I am.

With that, I knew what to write. Gingerly, I brought my fingers back to the keys.

Sometimes we forget. We stumble and fall when we become disconnected, when we think we are separate from the Creator. Our

73

purpose is to remember and experience the greatness that lives within each of us.

It's hard to put into words. I'm not used to sharing so much; it hasn't always been emotionally safe to do so. I know I can trust you. Thank you for encouraging me to open up!

Judi

Whether she knew it or not, Diana was the only one I could share these things with. I trusted her and I felt as though I could share openly without being judged. I began to look forward to our appointments more and more.

Over the following sessions, Diana seemed more open. And our email exchanges seemed increasingly nuanced and sensitive; she continued to probe me to go deeper, and she went deeper, herself. My incision wasn't hurting and the recovery was going well, so we began to look more seriously at the other issues in my life: my fears and my search for purpose. And that's how I found myself, just a few months after my first energy healing session, preparing for a past-life regression.

We started in the chairs, as always. I tried to explain some of my recent downloads, in particular one that explained that the spirits and guides I could feel were never there to hurt me; instead, they were divine gifts. Another that said *first we need to decide, and then the path unfolds.* We don't get to see the path and then decide whether to take it; change requires risking the unknown. During a third moment, looking out into the snow in the backyard, I found myself suddenly marveling at the beauty of it. It was as if I had never seen snow before. I felt how joyful it is to experience something as if for the first time, experiencing the sense of joy, wonder, and gratitude for every moment of life. I suddenly realized that *we can harness that joy always—whether it's actually the first time or not.* In a fourth download, I found myself speaking words I could never have crafted on my own in response to a question Diana asked about the greater meaning of violent crime: "We open our hearts with compassion and love for the victims and we come together as one—the one that we are all intended to be." I saw that *this union gives even something as horrific as violence a greater meaning*.

These things are couched in words, but they were so much more than that to me; they were feelings that moved through my body, sudden emotions that welled up and released back to wherever they came from, leaving behind only blessings. I struggled to write them down quickly, before they disappeared, but I didn't always have the ability to do so because they would suddenly arise in random moments, jarring me out of whatever I was trying to do in my earthly life. So I used the sessions with Diana to explain them as much as I could.

As I enumerated my recent downloads that day, Diana listened as if she understood the essence of what I was saying, even if the specific messages didn't prompt the same emotional response in her. I knew that experiencing and sharing them was part of my purpose. She agreed. "It's not just the words you received," she said, "but the energy of them. And you will likely keep receiving more of them."

We finished speaking and I knew it was time for the past-life regression. On a very basic level, I knew what to expect. Diana had prepared me by pointing me toward Dr. Brian Weiss, a leading past-life regressionist. Yet in terms of specifics, I had no idea what was about to take place. What would be revealed about my past lives? What might I see?

As I moved toward the table, she told me not to be afraid, but of course I was. I lay on the table and closed my eyes as she counted backwards from ten.

As my body relaxed, a color emerged in my mind. It had no shape or form, arising as a soft, purple haze. I felt myself drifting upwards, higher and higher, until I came through the haze and into a bright light. As my body reached the light, a feeling of love overpowered me. I was aware that on one level, my body was still on the table and in the room with Diana. But there was another level of existence, too, and in this dimension, I was surrounded. I merged with this feeling of love.

There, held in the love of God and the Universe, I received a poignant download: *You can always come home.* I understood that we can always return to the divine being of who we are and the greatness that lives within each of us. We can always go home by accepting who we are, loving who we are.

Back at the level of my body, my eyes filled with tears and overflowed. Slowly, I opened them as my body began to shake. I lay there, sobbing uncontrollably.

Diana was there, looking at me. She seemed concerned, though Spencer stayed asleep and didn't move. I tried to explain what had happened, but what can words do to describe something like that? "We can always just go home," I told her. "All we have to do is remember who we truly are. So many of us have forgotten.

"The remembering—it's joyful. The joy ... it's in the reunion, in the realization of who we are."

From his bed, Spencer sighed contentedly. As soon as I heard that sound, I knew that Diana understood.

I walked to the foyer a few minutes later, Diana at my side. Though I had not remembered a specific past life during our regression, I felt that perhaps I had remembered the place between lives once again, just as I had done on Good Friday. Furthermore, for just a second, I had communicated it successfully. Perhaps this knowing and this communication were part of my purpose.

As Diana turned to hug me goodbye, I suddenly found myself clinging to her. Everything I was seeing, hearing, and experiencing seemed beyond this world and yet here we were, living on Earth. These moments of clarity were so profound that it was hard to make sense of them in the context of the rest of my life. I clutched at Diana, overcome with emotion. I needed to hold onto something solid. I needed to know that these experiences were real.

As she validated my ongoing experiences, I began to trust Diana more and more. We continued to search for the details of my purpose. Shortly after the past-life regression, we moved to work on my *hara*.

I arrived at the session expecting it to be like any other. Spencer greeted me, and I spent several minutes connecting with him before he looked to Diana for approval and went to lie down. I sat back in the recliner as Diana explained the haric healing to me. She insisted upon doing this, but I found it slightly strange; as per her request, I had already read about haric healings in *Light Emerging* in advance of our meeting.

Barbara Brennan's teaching expands the Japanese idea of the hara, the power center in the lower belly. The haric level has everything to do with the reason we came here and it holds our deeper spiritual purpose. Within it are three vertical points along the center line of the body:

- one above the head, which represents our original individuation from God and carries our reason to incarnate;
- a second in the upper chest area, which corresponds to both our emotions and our sacred, spiritual longing that leads us through life and gives us the passion we need to complete our life task;
- and a third in the low belly, which houses our will to live in the physical body.

Once these three points are aligned, the reason for our incarnation unites with our drive to complete our life task while in a physical body. This, essentially, connects us to our purpose.

Most people are out of alignment in one way or another; they don't fully know their purpose, they don't know how to enact it, or they simply don't want to do so because on some level, they don't want to be in a physical body. Their decisions, therefore, reflect this misalignment. This means that aligning the haric line invariably brings a lot of life change in a short period of time. It may shift where we live, cause a career change, and even change our relationships on a fundamental level.

Diana looked at me sharply as she said this, making sure I was still listening. As we return to our true life's path, she explained, everything in the material world that doesn't serve our purpose either changes or drops away.

From the perspective of the healing, Diana explained, haric healing is quite advanced. As a Barbara Brennan healer, Diana had worked extensively to align and hold her own haric level before she was trained in aligning anyone else's. To do the haric healing, she would ground deeply into the earth and use her haric line to adjust the points on mine—without letting it knock her out of alignment. Because of this, and because I had to maintain my own alignment, I would have to remain perfectly still during the session, allowing her to move my body as necessary. I nodded that I understood. None of this information was new to me; it was precisely what I had read previously.

I was getting a little annoyed with her insistence on repeating this information. I felt as though I was ready to receive the healing; it was exactly what I needed. It seemed obvious that the haric healing was serious, and I couldn't understand why she felt the need to hammer that in so completely.

"So, understanding all of this, do you want to receive a haric healing?" she asked.

I nodded.

In any other circumstances, we would have both stood up and moved to the healing table. But that day, Diana stayed put, looking at me intently. "Do you really want to know what your purpose is?" she asked.

I told her I did. Of course, I wanted to know. I had been telling her for weeks that I desperately wanted to know what my purpose was. A haric healing was the obvious answer for how to figure it out, so why were we not proceeding?

She repeated her question. I looked right at her and answered again that yes, I did want to know what my purpose was. As I answered, she sat back in her chair, peering at me as if she were evaluating my response.

Spencer sighed. I felt like doing the same.

Diana finally said that if I wanted a haric healing, I would have to ask for it. Honestly, I was exasperated at this point. We had scheduled this session specifically for the haric healing and now she was telling me I had to ask for it. My communication wasn't always the clearest, but surely there was no miscommunication here. She had never made me ask for a healing before and I wasn't sure why she was making me do so now. In response to my silence, she repeated her request.

Exasperated, I heard myself ask, "Diana, may I have a haric healing, please?"

She held my gaze for a few long moments, then decisively said, "Yes."

We moved to the table.

As I lay quietly, I started by opening to gratitude, imagining the people I loved, and allowing my heart chakra to relax its defenses. Then, with my eyes shut, I began to scan the room with my other senses. I heard Spencer's soft breath, Diana's gentle footsteps, and the quiet rattle of her bracelets. I smelled the light essential oils from the hallway diffuser and, as Diana approached, the sweet floral scent that accompanied her. I felt the table below me and my body sinking onto it. I felt the way the fabrics of my clothes settled across my skin. Then, I felt her hands. Gently, she put her hands on my right calf and lifted my leg. She pressed it against her solar plexus.

Just then, Spencer jumped up from the floor. He began to race around the room—whether agitated or excited, I couldn't tell. I listened as Diana opened the door, still holding my leg, and gently pushed Spencer out into the foyer with her foot. I lay there with my eyes closed to hold the rest of my body still, thinking how strange the event was. Spencer never did that, as we both knew.

As she turned back toward me, Spencer began to frantically scratch at the door. He was desperate to get back into the room—whether to be with her or with me, or perhaps to be with both of us. Diana let this go on for some time before apologizing as she let him back in. It did no good; he began to leap up toward the table, trying to get on it *with* me.

In previous sessions, Spencer would shift around on his bed from time to time, but mostly he slept. I had never before noticed him agitated. He had certainly never done anything like that before.

My head began to tingle as I lay on the table, Diana still trying to perform the haric healing while Spencer continued to jump at the table. I have no idea how many minutes went on like this—thirty, forty-five, maybe longer. Spencer remained wild the entire time, trying to get to me on the table. Diana pushed through until the haric healing was complete, and then she ended the session, apologizing for Spencer's behavior even though I never would have blamed her.

I was dumbfounded. Why would he act so strangely? What type of energy was he sensing in the room? What divine beings had entered and what were they there to do? What was happening during the haric healing that agitated him so?

As soon as I got off the table, Spencer calmed and lay down on his bed, back to his friendly, mellow self. I went to pat his head gently and he wagged his tail. Whatever he sensed had subsided, and he settled down once again.

Diana walked me to the door and I hugged her goodbye.

Retrospect is everything. At the time I asked for the haric healing— and Diana made quite sure that I asked for it—I didn't fully understand what it meant. Despite the reading I had done and our conversation that day, there are some things we have to experience to understand. And I certainly could not have predicted what it would go on to mean or what the ramifications would be. This is often true of deep healing: we know we want change, but we aren't always ready for what that looks like. Though the Universe always answers us, it's not always in the way we expect, and the consequences of our own evolution often go beyond what we can imagine.

I see now that during the haric healing, the separate paths that my soul and Diana's soul had been traversing merged into one. Our haras aligned and from that point forward, we were connected. Or perhaps we were always connected, but now, our connection was no longer a choice.

Prior to the haric healing, I believed I had a choice to stop going to see Diana. But after that session took place, I felt that we were forever linked: our purpose together clicked into place. At the time, I didn't know yet that Diana had a deep connection to my family, so it was an odd feeling. I cared for Diana, but I felt somewhat ambivalent about this fusing of our paths and our destinies.

After the haric healing, Diana and I had a few more sessions dedicated to the search for my purpose. But as much as I looked forward to seeing Diana (and Spencer) week after week, I couldn't justify these visits as "healing" anymore.

By the time Diana and I did the haric healing, my incision only hurt on occasion. I was walking about two miles a day and was able to perform most basic activities. According to the doctors, I was "healed." The logical part of my mind took this to mean it was time to be finished with Diana, too. Searching for purpose and looking for validation for the increasingly confusing spiritual occurrences in my life didn't seem like a strong enough reason to continue seeing her.

Our connection was undeniable. Yet did I really *need* her? I couldn't make sense of why I was there anymore. I knew our work together had been important, and I certainly *wanted* to keep going, but I no longer knew what I was going to receive. As much as I disliked the idea, as I prepared for my first week back at the office, I began to think it was time for my work with Diana to come to an end. Somehow, I would have to find a way to say goodbye.

Chapter Six

Alone

Three months after the hysterectomy, it was time for me to return to work. I still didn't fully understand my purpose, but I was closer to it. And honestly, I felt I wouldn't have time to keep up with the healing sessions with Diana. The long days in the office combined with the work I took home on the evenings and weekends and the nearly two hours I spent daily in my car left few extra hours for anything else.

At the same time, I knew I needed someone to help me understand everything that was happening to me. No one else in my world could understand. It seemed like there was no one I could be totally open and vulnerable with, no one who would understand my downloads without judgment. I felt as though I was being pulled by a force outside myself to continue the sessions. But did I have enough time to dedicate to them, given the daily demands of my life?

This quandary was the one thing I felt I couldn't discuss with Diana. I wasn't sure she would understand, and I didn't want to hurt her feelings. We came from such different worlds. How could she understand the pressures of my job or the isolation I felt from the people around me?

My intuition told me to continue seeing her, but my logic couldn't make sense of it. Logic began to win over. My mind became so loud I couldn't hear the intuition anymore, and I didn't know what to do.

As I prepared to return to work, I realized Diana's and my schedules would no longer align. It felt like the decision had been made for me. Though Diana had always gone above and beyond to make time for our sessions, it just didn't seem reasonable to ask her to do so any longer. So, the week before I returned to work, I scheduled my final session with her.

It was an unremarkable session in most respects. Spencer remained calm; Diana remained her supportive self. Like so many times before, I was struck by how *myself* I felt; somehow, it was easier to be authentic and open within the four walls of her office than nearly anywhere else.

As I sat in the yellow recliner at the end of the session, I wanted to tell Diana that I loved her and that she had touched me deeply. I wanted to express how much impact she'd had on my life. We're so often terrified of those three little words, "I love you." We focus on the surface concerns: That they'll be misinterpreted or will bring some sort of pressure to the recipient. But underneath that, it's the vulnerability that scares us. The same yearning that causes us to love someone pulls us away from them, too; we simultaneously want, and don't want, for our hearts to be seen.

It's when the walls come down and we expose our hearts that we truly live. But taking the walls apart is sometimes scary. Though love is meant to be shared, we hoard it.

I wished desperately that I could tell her how I truly felt. But once again, expression eluded me and the words wouldn't come. I sat in the yellow recliner, unable to use my voice. On his bed, Spencer watched me intently. So, I thanked Diana for everything. I said some things that were generic but, I hoped, poignant.

Then I reached down into my bag for the gift I had brought her: a glass sphere filled with sand and seashells from the same beach near where my father's ashes lie. I intuitively knew that she loved the beach, and the symbolism of my father's resting place was rich for me. I handed it to her, hoping it could say everything that I could not. On the floor, Spencer shifted and sighed as Diana smiled and thanked me for the gift, telling me she loved the beach and asking how I knew. *Of course, I knew*, I thought. We were somehow connected.

The day I said goodbye to Diana, I could not find the words to tell her I loved her, so I gave her the sand globe instead.

The following weeks were the most challenging I had experienced in a long time. Once again, I was back in the world of ten-hour workdays that were, somehow, never long enough to do everything I needed to do. The backlog of leftover items from my leave was impossible to get through, and I felt as though I was running after a train as it sped up on the tracks, falling a little bit further behind each day that went by. Just like before, I brought my work home with me and worked into the night after dinner. I spent my weekends catching up and preparing for the next week. My commute felt longer than ever, the landscape barren in the dark and heavy winter. I slept less, walked less, and fought to keep some connection with myself in whatever spare time I had.

I had always enjoyed my job. I had long known that I worked too much, but it wasn't until after I returned from medical leave that I could really see the repercussions. I had grown accustomed to slow, methodical movement, abundant rest, and time to reflect while reading and listening to spiritual teachers. I no longer had any time for that, except for the podcasts and audiobooks I could listen to during my daily commute. At home, my days had been relatively happy—even if many of them were deeply physically painful—and drama free. Now, the drama was turned up to high volume, as office politics and power struggles continued. I found myself watching these from the sideline, reluctant to participate unless it was absolutely necessary. I knew what such participation would cost me, both emotionally and physically, and I no longer understood what there was to gain from it. I wondered why I had even participated in the first place. Was it to prove myself? I had been proving myself in the office for over twenty-five years—when would enough be enough? I now understood that I was already worthy; like everyone else, I had been born worthy. So what was there to prove? For years, I had operated under the subconscious assumption that things would be better, more efficient, or more productive if I controlled everything.

I let go of this control and life became easier. I understood that what we resist persists, so I just stopped resisting.

This process was challenging. I had an easy viewpoint from which to understand the transformation I had undergone in recent months. It was clear that the version of myself that had gone on medical leave was not the version of myself that had returned from it. But while I was pleased with how I had grown, the changes in me made my everyday life much harder. There was a battle going on between the being I had become and the life that being had to live—a battle I was losing. I began to feel myself slowly fading away.

Without Diana, I had no one to remind me of everything I had experienced. I had no one to tell me if I was going astray or to lead me back toward my true self. I had gone from long discussions about purpose to the rat race of trying to prove oneself, move ahead, and make money—goals I no longer shared. I didn't want to fall back into old patterns, valuing the wrong things and fighting for my place in the world. I wanted to be in the flow instead.

But getting to that flow was going to take time. During my early morning drives, I began relistening to old self-help favorites. I found myself gravitating more and more toward spiritual authors like Wayne Dyer, Kyle Gray, and Esther Hicks. After work was finished, I would put on my favorite playlists and sing. In truth, I'm slightly tone deaf, but inside my car there's no one else to hear me. With less time to practice the classical guitar, I used the vibration of my voice to open my heart, returning me to the memory of who I had become when Diana was by my side. As the demands of work and regular life pulled me under, my drives became my practice; they supplanted meditation, exercising, playing music, and being in nature. When I had the energy,

I would listen to Sonia Choquette's guided meditations at night, allowing myself to feel everything she described. I hoped it would be enough.

Every once in a while, I would receive a spiritual download. These were still spontaneous, but I noticed that they mostly came in times when I was quiet and alone—times when it was safe enough for my heart to remain open. These times came fewer and further between, but they still came, and true to form, poignant downloads accompanied them.

Yet without context, it was harder to hold on to the wisdom they contained. *The answers lie within us; we do not need to search outside of ourselves.* I knew this was true, but I also knew I needed support; I couldn't trust myself for all the answers. *Trust in the Universe. There is nothing you do not know or cannot do.* But clearly, existing as an accounting professional and a spiritual being simultaneously *was* something I couldn't do—wasn't it?

As my loneliness increased without Diana, the downloads began to address it directly. *The loneliness and emptiness are when you become disconnected from Source and the essence of who you truly are. The loneliness is the longing to be reconnected and reunited with the oneness of all that we are.* But *how?*, I asked myself. *How do we reconnect when we're so exhausted all the time?* I let myself ask these questions, knowing that by doing so I was opening myself to receive.

One morning as I drove to work, I listened to a lecture by Dolores Cannon, the author of *The Convoluted Universe* series of books.

Diana had recommended these books to me before I went back to work. It was on the border of my comfort zone already; Dolores Cannon would hypnotize her clients and do past-life regressions in which her clients spoke of different lifetimes, different dimensions, and even different planets.

These ideas were completely new to me. I found myself fascinated. At the same time, I knew that if I couldn't share something like the idea that we have past lives with the people close to me, I surely couldn't share the idea that we may have experienced them in other dimensions. The more I was pulled toward this new world, the more I felt the power of the Universe surrounding and supporting me, the more I felt alienated from the humans in my reality.

The lecture continued as I considered all of this. Then, Dolores Cannon began to speak about the immense knowledge we are given and our power to use it for incredible good or evil. She explained that our understanding of atomic energy is a gift from the divine. Just our ability to comprehend how energy moves, how atoms split and interact, despite the fact that we could never see it with our own eyes, is itself a miracle. And instead of using this knowledge for good, we used it to destroy. We created the atomic bomb, which killed thousands, scorched the earth, and caused untold suffering. We created nuclear power, which was as dangerous as it was beyond our control. We had used an immense gift of knowledge against each other and the earth we live upon.

Listening to her speak, I began to cry. I don't cry often, but there I was, unable to stop myself. I thought about all I had been given and what I had done with it. I was afraid of my own power. I knew it. The spiritual gifts I was given also felt like they came with an overwhelming responsibility. I wanted to take care of what the Creator had given me. I wanted to be a good steward. That's part of why I wanted to know my purpose—and the exact reason that, deep down, I was afraid to do so. I didn't want to truly understand my life's purpose, because if I did, I would be out of excuses. In taking ownership over what I was here to do, I would have to actually *do* it.

And would I? Could I? Would I have the courage to do so? What if this capacity for evil that Dolores Cannon spoke about won out?

Somehow, I pulled myself together and parked my car at work.

I sat with this fear all day, braving the office while secretly feeling even less connected inside. Then, on my drive home, I let myself sing it out. I sang some of my favorites, including "Let It Be" by the Beatles. After a few minutes, my ambivalence subsided. I received the download,

You cannot be what you are not. I knew that my essence was love. Yes, I was powerful, but I would use it for good. There was nothing to fear.

I wish I could say that this particular download stuck with me, but like so many others, it came and went in a flash. I remembered the words and tried to hold onto the emotional experience, but the actual feeling of it moved through me and was gone.

Though my fascination with learning about past lives had been growing for a while, my experience while listening to Dolores Cannon that day made me increasingly interested in this work. The idea that someone could remember a past life drew me in; it challenged my idea of what "dead" was in the first place.

The way I saw it, people in my daily life had a much narrower view on what was spiritual and what was not, and they tended to restrict what is real and possible to what they had seen with their own eyes. These ideas just weren't accepted, and as a result, they weren't very *acceptable.* As I listened to talks and books on the subject of past lives, I became more and more aware that I needed to hide my interest. These ideas seemed to be on the fringe of what most people could accept, and I didn't want anyone to discount me for believing—or at least, refusing to *disbelieve*—what these teachers and authors were saying.

I didn't know if it was all real. But at the same time, what if? What if it were true? Wouldn't the wisdom someone gained on their journey be worthy of listening to, even if it came from a past life?

I became incredibly interested in how understanding and integrating the lessons from our past lives could help us heal what we suffer from in this lifetime. I watched an interview in which Dr. Brian Weiss explained how he came to believe in past lives in the first place. In a regular hypnosis session with one particular client, he saw her heal from inexplicable phobias that had caused her to suffer since childhood. She did this by recounting the past-life experiences that had planted the seed for each of her fears.

What about my strange and unfounded fears? Could there be a past-life connection that I just had not accessed yet? And if so, could I be healed?

These were the thoughts and experiences that led me to attend a local workshop that Dr. Weiss was leading. When I arrived at the event center, I was shocked by what I saw. There were probably over a thousand people in the room—all of whom looked entirely normal. They were average, regular people like me. The sheer number of them was what struck me; it meant that these ideas were resonating with far more people than I had ever thought.

Though I had been interested in Dr. Weiss, I had not done much research on him beyond my initial google search. I knew he was famous within his own niche, but I had no idea that his work was so popular on a broader scale. Looking at the swarm of people around me, I realized how reputable past-life regression really was.

Beyond that, actually having a past-life experience was also less uncommon than I had previously believed. As part of his introduction, Dr. Weiss explained that he would do three or four hypnoses on the crowd. Within each of these, he estimated that half of us would have a past-life regression at some point that day. That meant hundreds of people would remember a past life. I found this to be extraordinary. I knew his confidence was born from experience, and I found it to be quite convincing.

The lights dimmed. Most people sat in chairs, but a few dozen of us lay down on yoga mats. We made ourselves comfortable and the room got quiet. Then Dr. Weiss began to speak.

After some basic visualization, he began to take us up to a series of doors. Each door corresponded to a period in history, and we were told to enter the door that called out to us. Nothing called out to me. Finally, he got to the last door and said that this door was for everyone who was left. Still lying on the floor, I opened it and felt myself cautiously step in.

I don't know what happened next; there is a total break in my memory. I only heard a gentle breath that grew louder and louder over time.

As Dr. Weiss began to guide us awake, I realized I had been listening to the sound of my own snoring.

Somehow, I had slept through the entire thing!

I was disappointed to realize that I was one of the participants who had *not* had a past-life regression. Just like my experience with Diana, in which I had perhaps emotionally remembered the space between lives but not remembered the details of a past life, I was crushed to find that once again, my past lives had eluded me. My sense of disappointment was palpable. I wandered through the crowd, looking at the faces around me. *So many of these people remembered a past life today*, I thought. *Why not me?*

Before leaving, I purchased one of Dr. Weiss's audio hypnoses. Over the coming weeks, I listened to it again and again. Despite my conviction, my body fell asleep every single time. I was frustrated and exhausted. Why couldn't I stay awake? Why couldn't I remember my own past lives and get to the heart of my fears?

The fears I had experienced since childhood were no better, despite the work I had done. I was still afraid of the dark. Secretly, within this fear was housed the completely irrational fear of sexual assault. Though the work with Diana had opened me somewhat, it still had been hard for me to let her touch my body without at least some small bit of tension rising within me. Even in our later sessions, after months of working together, I had lain there with my eyes shut tightly as my body slowly relaxed over the course of each healing.

I was afraid of being discovered, too. I didn't want to know what my friends and family—or, heaven forbid, my colleagues—would think of me if they found out what I was listening to or studying. The downloads, intuitions, perceptions, and gifts I had received were relegated to the shadows in my day-to-day life. I wanted to stay hidden, I didn't want to be seen. No one could understand—maybe not even Diana. I thought back to our early sessions when she had asked me repeatedly about a history of hospitalization. Over and over again, I told her that no, I had never been hospitalized long-term or had major issues. This had barely fazed me at the time, but thinking back, I wondered whether she had been referring to hospitalization for mental, not physical health. Though I often tried to push it away, the idea haunted me; if I couldn't trust her to understand me, how could I trust anyone? The fear of social rejection and all the consequences that accompany it nagged at me.

New fears cropped up, too.

One morning, I was lying in bed after my alarm had gone off. Suddenly, I felt the presence of a spirit. Though I didn't visualize him with my eyes, I knew what he looked like—or, specifically, I knew about one feature, which was so overwhelming I could not see anything else. While the face around them blurred out of view, his dark, oval eyes terrorized me. They were the deepest black I had ever seen; they felt completely unhuman. The being peered at me with the enormous, dark hollows of his eyes as I lay paralyzed. As soon as I could, I jumped out of bed and cleared my head. But the memory of his stare haunted me.

I was also still wrestling with the question of my own power that had arisen when I listened to Dolores Cannon speak about atomic energy. It seemed like every bit of spiritual growth carried increased responsibility. I knew I had to use the wisdom I gained for good, but what if I couldn't do that?

These thoughts bounced around in my head, with no one to talk to and no support. I missed Diana. I missed the version of myself who had sat in that yellow recliner. I missed Spencer. I missed the conviction that accompanied my downloads. I missed the joyful, kind guides who had helped me through so much. I missed feeling understood.

In those few long months, despite everything that I knew about the Universe, I felt completely alone.

Chapter Seven

The Truth

The phone rang. I saw Miriam's name on the screen. I often felt torn when my mother-in-law called; I loved her, and in some ways we were close. She and I had certainly learned how to be family in the many years of my marriage, which coincided exactly with the years she had spent as a widow after Paul's death. Those early years were marked by transition for both of us, and we had learned to adapt to our new roles together. But Miriam and I had always struggled in some ways, too; her kindness and generosity often seemed to have the secondary aim of leading me to be more like her. The clothes she bought for me were totally not my style; the stereotypical feminine activities she suggested, like shopping or going to the salon, were things I would never do for fun. As I perceived it, there was a judgment in these actions; I felt that she was trying to make me more like who she was, instead of loving me as I was. I knew that I was different. But did she see me? Did she recognize who I was and hope that I would change, or did she misunderstand me completely?

I felt guilty for having these feelings, especially in recent months because she had been sick. I truly cared for Miriam and didn't want her to suffer. As soon as I heard her voice, I knew that her time was coming; it felt like she was already somewhat not in this world.

"We need to go visit your mom," I told my husband a few minutes later. "Now."

"Are you sure?" he responded nervously. Discussing a parent's death is never an easy conversation. "She didn't ask us to come. And the kids are in school; we would have to pull them out. Do you really think it's an emergency? I talked to my sister and …"

"Your mother is not going to ask," I said firmly. "But if we want our kids to see their grandmother before she passes, now is the time."

We flew out the next day. Sometimes I just know things, and this time, I was right. It was well after dark when we arrived at the assisted living facility where Miriam lived and we stayed until midnight, telling her we would return in the morning. I reached over and kissed my mother-in-law on the forehead and told her that I loved her. As we left, she drifted off to sleep. She never woke again.

Miriam passed away before any other long-distance family members arrived, but my husband, our kids, and I were lucky enough to have a chance to say goodbye. As sad as I was, I was grateful I listened to my intuition and pushed my husband to listen to it, too.

I had already been feeling alone, and I had no idea how strongly the force of her passage would hit me. In the days following her death, I grieved Miriam deeply. On the outside, I probably seemed completely put together, just going through the motions of preparing for the funeral and trying to provide emotional support for the rest of the family. But inside, I was filled with an overwhelming sense of sadness, and thinking of Miriam constantly. I realized that grief is an emotion that can move very slowly—it can take a long time to release. When I allowed myself to be present with my grief it swelled up within me and threatened to burst.

I was lying in bed during one of these swells when I began to develop a strange sensation that I wasn't just thinking about Miriam; I was communicating with her directly. As soon as I recognized this, a giant movie screen appeared before my eyes. I suddenly saw dozens of interactions between me and my husband's family flash by in an instant. The rapid progression of scenes jolted me to attention, and then just as suddenly, the movie screen disappeared. The scenes themselves were rather mundane, but the message they held for me was clear: *I had made myself different from the rest of the family, clinging to how I had been judged and wronged, and building an iron barrier around my heart to close it off and protect myself from the world.* I knew without a doubt that this visual and emotional message had come directly from Miriam.

She had not misunderstood me or tried to change me. And she certainly had not judged me. To the contrary, *I* was the one who had judged the situation by assuming that no one could accept me for my differences. I had tried to protect myself from the negativity I perceived in her, and as a result I had not received the positivity she had offered. She took me to get my nails done and bought me flowy, feminine blouses because those were the things she loved and she was trying to share them with me. She wasn't trying to reject me; she was trying to embrace me with the things she held most dear. In all the years that I had known her, I had never seen this. It was all my projection because what we project is mirrored back to us, and what we see is therefore just the reflection of ourselves.

I lay awake with my breath still caught in my throat, knowing that like many of the healings and downloads I had received in recent months, this experience would mark me forever. I began to cry uncontrollably as I felt the gratitude for what she had taught me, not in life but in death. I missed Miriam terribly, yet I knew that she had given me the greatest gift she could give; one that would forever be imprinted on my heart. I continued to sob and as I fell asleep, the download arrived: *Love is never too late, even in death.*

When I arrived home, I wanted desperately to share this with someone, but who could understand? My husband was grieving and had shown little interest in the things that were changing in me. My kids already thought I was weird and told me so freely. There was barely time to discuss personal things in the Your Year of Miracles calls, and most of my days at work were spent with colleagues who were always too busy.

I wanted to tell Diana.

Something deep inside nagged at me, insisting that my story with Diana was not complete. Whatever had opened during the haric healing confirmed something that I had intuitively suspected: She and I were connected, our stories were intertwined. With Diana, some loose end was just hanging there, waiting to be tied.

The problem was that I didn't know exactly, *what* it was.

But I knew that I missed Diana. Since the gift Miriam had given me in death, I was coming to understand love in a whole new way.

Downloads continued to arrive, telling me *love is the one infinite resource that we can constantly give away and that will always be there to give again; it's only for us to allow it.* I didn't know what to do with these, so I wrote them in my journal. This guidance was teaching me not only about love itself, but about my relationship to love—essentially, that *I am love. You do not have to prove you are lovable, for you are already divine love,* I scrawled on a blank journal page. *You are the light, the love, the infinite power of all that is, was, and ever will be.* My heart continued to open as I learned that *love transcends all time and space.*

Though they were often centered in the heart, I felt these downloads throughout my entire body. In their perfect truth, they were not only verbal experiences made of words, but emotional experiences made of feeling.

I realized that Miriam had been able to show me my projection precisely because I was feeling these feelings. And I knew I was not alone in that understanding; these were cerebral conversations that I'd had with Diana, the truth of which I was now experiencing in real time. I wanted to tell her about them. She was the only one I could think of who might possibly understand.

I also wanted to tell her about the dichotomy of experiencing these spiritual truths, living and breathing through these divine downloads, while still facing so much struggle on the physical plane. How could someone who knew all that I knew still be so afraid? I was once again sleeping with the bathroom light on because the fear that gripped me at night was paralyzing. You know that feeling when someone jumps out in front of you? For most people, it only lasts a few seconds, but for me it could last for hours. I didn't want to see the dark-eyed being from my vision again, nor any other scary, disembodied thing that could be lurking in the night. My fear tugged at me as though the darkness might open its mouth and consume me whole—and what if it did, metaphorically speaking? What if I became a dark being myself, using my rediscovered spiritual power for harm?

As these thoughts took up more and more space in my head, I put less and less energy into certain aspects of my work. I was still scrambling to catch up from my time off, which was understandable given my workload. I barely had time for my favorite things outside of work, such as playing the classical guitar and walking around the reservoir. The best way for me to open my heart was to sing during my commute, when I wasn't listening to spiritual audiobooks.

I was nearly as productive as ever, but I no longer cared about the parts of work that weren't directly about *doing the work*. I didn't care to prove myself, I didn't care to step over others to ensure my own rise, and I didn't care to drain myself completely in order to be some sort of superstar. I was still working long hours, but I had stopped playing politics. I had stopped playing altogether. In terms of my actual work, the shift was barely perceivable. I continued to produce reports, present at events, and lead a large team. In fact, I probably came off as happier and more easygoing at work.

But people feel energy, and it didn't take long for my boss to feel mine.

The day he pulled me into his office, I honestly had no idea what was about to happen. I thought that we would once again review a management presentation or discuss some detailed aspect of work. He looked at me, cheery and smiling, and told me they had found a new position for me.

"A new position?" I asked. I had not applied for a lateral move, nor had I even been considering it. Looking back, I was entirely innocent. I honestly thought that if I brought my best self to the corporate world, I would be rewarded.

He explained the "new position," which sounded and felt like a demotion to me. I went from leading a team of fifty to overseeing a single employee in a matter of minutes.

I left his office dejected and confused.

Everything is a reflection of me—but how was *this* a reflection of me? Spiritually, I had *grown*! But professionally, I had, what ... *shrunk*? Plus, I was just back and now able to work from the office more regularly, whereas bleeding from uterine cysts had put me working from home intermittently for months.

The hysterectomy had mostly healed that. Certainly, the fibroids were gone. But in recent weeks I had begun to bleed a little here and there. With Miriam's death and my desperate attempt to catch up at work, I had not had time to address it. When it finally became severe, I did go to see Dr. Daniels, but she couldn't find anything wrong. So on and off, I continued to bleed.

As I drove home the night of my "demotion," a sharp, stabbing pain began to radiate from my abdomen. By the time I got home it was undeniable: Something was wrong.

I went to the emergency room and ended up staying for nine hours. During that time, the doctors ran multiple tests but could find nothing; all they could say was that the pain was probably coming from my ovaries and that from a medical standpoint, everything was fine.

I knew in my heart that the person who could help me was Diana. Her work to remove blockages from my aura could only help the bleeding, not hurt it. And it would help so much more, too, with the fears that were pulling me into darkness, the grief at losing Miriam, and the anger and confusion I felt about the shifts at work.

The next day, I sat at my computer. "Dear Diana ..."

She encouraged me to come in for another session almost immediately. As soon as I was seated again in the yellow recliner, Spencer was curled up on his bed, and Diana was poised in her straight-backed chair, I knew that everything would be all right. I poured out everything that had happened in the time I had not seen her: Miriam's death, the downloads, the hollow-eyed presence, and the spike in my ever-present fight against fear. She listened intently. When I got to the part about my job—something that was still hard to talk about without becoming emotional—she leaned forward, listening with compassion. For the first time in many weeks, I felt understood.

I continued to see Diana regularly. I knew that working with her was no longer an option. After our second week together, I received a download that confirmed it: *You do not need to be in pain to need healing.* Sure enough, the bleeding subsided. Had it all been part of my body's push to get me back on Diana's healing table?

Once again, Diana and I dove headlong into my fears. She asked me numerous questions about my past, trying to figure out why I was afraid of things like darkness. I still had not told her about the accompanying fear of sexual assault. "Can you think back to a moment in time when you were afraid?" she would ask. "What was happening around you? What were you seeing, sensing, feeling, saying to yourself?" I answered these questions as honestly as I could but the connection to my past seemed sketchy enough to be nonexistent.

During every session we would devote at least a little time to my purpose. Accounting, while it was something I enjoyed and was honestly quite good at, was clearly not the reason I was put on this Earth. And that was confirmed when showing up to work with my heart open only served to punish me. Diana seemed almost as committed as I was to finding my purpose. Midway through our search, I began to wonder what would happen when I found it. Thus far, I had not proven to be very effective at accepting the gifts I had been given. I wondered if when I found my purpose, I would be afraid to admit it aloud.

Meanwhile, I was listening to more and more about past-life regressions. Seeing Dr. Brian Weiss—and seeing the crowd who followed him—gave this sort of work a mainstream legitimacy that made it more attractive to me. Diana recommended that I check out Michael Newton, PhD, who used hypnosis to explore the afterlife through his clients. I loved listening to the interviews that he, Dr. Brian Weiss, and

Dolores Cannon conducted, discussing the reports from people in a hypnotized state who would speak about their past lives in other times and even other worlds.

I was driving home from work one day, admiring the green leaves returning after a long winter, when I heard an interview that shocked me. One of Michael Newton's interviewees, deep in hypnosis, had a guide speak through him. Michael asked his client how else the guide communicated, and he answered that the guide often whispered in the ears of the humans he was guiding—exactly as my Irish nurse, the male voice who helped me play the guitar, and the many guides who offered me downloads did with me. Then he and Michael began to discuss a type of spirit that showed itself with "black, glowing cavities for eyes." I was shocked; this was exactly what I had seen in bed one morning a few weeks before! This being's hollow eyes had haunted me, but Michael Newton's interviewee explained that they aren't exactly eyes; they represent a concentrated intensity of thought and presence. He described them as "windows to old bodies" and "physical extensions to former selves."

I was relieved to hear that what I was sensing and experiencing was real, and I wasn't imagining it. Furthermore, I didn't have to be afraid.

I told Diana what I had heard in Michael Newton's interview as soon as I saw her next. Like always, she listened patiently. Then she remarked that it seemed quite validating. As with all the other experiences I had shared with her, she accepted it unconditionally.

This was what I had missed. *This* was what I needed. Diana affirmed my spiritual truths as just that: Truths. Whether they were objective truths didn't seem to matter. The fact that they were true to me was real enough for her.

I was so grateful to be seen that way. And I still felt somewhere deep inside of me that we were connected.

One day while we were discussing my fears, Diana suggested that she could hypnotize me to see if there were any formative experiences hiding in my subconscious. I was somewhat afraid of what I might say, but even more afraid that if something *were* hiding within me, summoning it to the surface would force me to relive it. Lying on the floor in a group format with Dr. Brian Weiss was one thing. Being directly asked questions by someone I considered a friend was another.

However, I agreed.

I lay on the table, breathing deeply, as Diana counted backwards. Then, fully awake, I felt myself enter the hypnotic trance. I was fully conscious and aware but unable to censor my words. I was surprised to see that I had no inhibitions about this; not only was I liable to say anything, I was no longer worried about that fact.

Diana asked me some basic questions and I heard my voice answering her, robotic and measured. Then she went deeper.

"Judi, what was your scariest encounter with a spirit?"

I found myself retelling a story I had completely forgotten. It was late one night, shortly after Paul's death. As I lay in bed, listening to Miriam crying in the next room, I wondered if I could ever love someone as much as she loved Paul. My worries about marriage began to converge around this single thought, *I loved my then-fiancé dearly, but would it be enough?* That night, I awoke to the presence of someone kneeling beside me. I could not move to see the being clearly; I was completely paralyzed by fear. Then, I heard a soft voice telling me that my marriage was meant to be; it was destined. This message proved to be true. But despite the warm and affirming message, my paralyzing fear made the event terrifying.

When my robotic voice finished relating this story, Diana asked another question. "When was the first time you saw a spirit?"

My mouth opened and I heard my own voice telling her that I was a young child—maybe eight years old—and home alone. I was walking down the hallway to my room when I saw a woman standing at the end of it, wearing a long dress and surrounded by gray and white shadows. She didn't try to communicate with me; in fact, she may not have noticed me at all. But she was deeply disturbing to me because she *floated.* As if she were made of air, she drifted through my parents' closed bedroom door and then through my own. I knew without a doubt that this was my father's mother who had died when he was a child. It was terrifying. I wasn't afraid that she would hurt me, but I was afraid of the power of what she could do—she could float between rooms and through doors—even, ostensibly, locked ones!

Slowly, Diana pulled me out of the hypnosis and I blinked in the light of her office. I was aware that this was where I had been the whole time. I was aware that I had not fallen asleep. But as I felt my conscious mind take control over my body, there was a profound difference between waking and the trance. I sat with that vulnerability for a minute.

We had not gotten to the bottom of my fears. But I had seen two memories I had suppressed in the past. I understood that my ancestors were with me, all the time, just like my guides. I was never alone. And somehow, I felt, these multiple factors—my fears, my ancestors, my purpose, and Diana—were linked.

As I drove home that day, I asked my guides to show me my purpose with a physical sign. It was hard for me to trust the things I felt; it was much easier to trust what I could see. And if I couldn't get to the heart of my fears, at least I hoped to figure out my purpose.

A few evenings later, I picked up *The (Not So) Little Book of Surprises* by Deirdre Hade and William Arntz.

A card fell out. I examined it closely, remembering that I had asked for a physical sign to show me my purpose. I looked at the card, but nothing on it resonated with me—at least, not enough to remember today. But I do remember what happened when I looked at the page from which it had fallen.

In the middle of the page, surrounded by other text, my eyes landed upon a single sentence. "And, what if you're someone who's coming in to bring the new words of the great Light Beings—the new words built on the old words, built on the ancient texts?"

Deirdre's words swirled in my mind. I thought back to the many downloads I had received. I felt the emotions of all I had experienced in the last year swell up and pass through me. *Observation creates the awareness that unlocks the understanding*, one download had told me, so I sat and observed everything I had learned.

And then, I received one of the biggest downloads of my life:

My purpose is to help people reawaken the Creator within so they can live the truest desires of their heart. And to embrace the love, joy, and wonder along the way.

I sat on the bed, breathing deeply and feeling this download move through me. It linked everything together—opening the heart, where we access the Creator, and finding the joy in the discovery. This was my purpose and it was perfect.

My journal was right beside me. I could have written it down. My tablet wasn't far away, either; I could have sent an email to Diana. I didn't.

Knowing my purpose felt joyful and exciting. I understood what all the downloads were there for—I was meant to share them through words, through expression, which was why I had been called to work so hard on my throat chakra.

But just as I had suspected, when I finally did find my purpose, I didn't want to own it. I didn't want to face the immensity of what it would mean if I did.

Slowly, I closed the book and crawled into bed. In the glow of the light coming through the bathroom door, I closed my eyes and went to sleep.

While there was nothing fun about my workdays, I spent them largely detached, working much harder in the spiritual realm and preparing for my mother's eightieth birthday party, which my siblings and I would be hosting the following weekend.

When the day of the party arrived, I was happy to gather with my extended family to celebrate my mother. She was the cornerstone of our family; she had taught us how to love unconditionally and be truly kind, and she was the moral compass who represented our shared values.

As the festivities began, I found myself connecting with my brother at the kitchen table. I was somewhat high on my spiritual growth and accessing gratitude was easy, so I began explaining in earnest how lucky we were to have a mother like her. She had always provided a safe and loving home for us; she had shown us, by example, how to give of one-self and be of service. My mother, in short, was a blessing.

My brother agreed, remarking that it was truly incredible given the extremely hard life she had lived. I was taken aback. I knew that her father had left when she was young and that things were not exactly easy for her in childhood. I also knew that she and my own father had worked very hard, both before and after immigrating from Trinidad. But from what I understood, I would not describe it as a particularly difficult life.

Then my brother told me a story I had never heard—in fact, I had never even heard anyone hint that something so horrible could possibly be true.

He explained that my mother had been raped by her mother's boy-friend, her *de facto* stepfather, at the age of twelve. While she lay in bed one night, he had entered the room and violated her. Not only that, but this violation impregnated her. To avoid the impending stigma and judgment, my mother—herself a child—had been whisked away to live out the pregnancy and give birth in secret. Not even her own siblings knew the truth. The baby was given up for adoption and her mother, my grandmother, forbade her to ever speak of it again.

In the days before my father's death, my brother had been told the truth. As the oldest child, he had been entrusted with our family secret.

I sat in horror, trying to imagine what my mother had gone through and how she had suffered. I had dozens of questions. What happened to the stepfather? Where was the baby—who was now likely an adult of sixty-seven? Why had my mother agreed to keep such a secret? How could this be true when my mother was so kind and gentle? How could her scars be so invisible?

Why had she not told us?

Our conversation was interrupted when my mother walked into the room. I stared at her, unable to comprehend the heinous thing she had lived through, while trying to disguise my shock as happiness as we celebrated her birthday. My brother and I barely said a word to each other for the rest of the party.

In the car on the way home, I longed to turn up the stereo and sing. But I was driving with my family, who were deep in a conversation about something else, totally unaware of what I now knew. Silently, I begged my heart to not close in reaction to this painful awareness. I implored it not to protect me from this.

As soon as I arrived back at my computer, I opened my inbox and began to compose an email. I wanted to write everything—but I couldn't.

"Dear Diana," I typed. "I know why I'm afraid of the dark."

Chapter Eight

The Revelation

After my mother's birthday party, everything began to happen very quickly. The revelation I experienced on Good Friday, the "click" I heard when I first met Diana, and the merging between her soul's purpose and my own during the haric healing were strong forces that came together, swirling in a cyclone that lifted Diana, my mother, and me to our shared destiny.

I only know this from hindsight, of course. As the events began to unfold, they all seemed much more worldly than that.

I kept replaying the scene that I had always thought to be a fear-based invention: There I was, lying in my bed, when a man entered my room and sexually assaulted me. Without my own story to attach to this living nightmare, it made no sense. But now, knowing my mother's story, perhaps it did.

At first, I was desperate to find out more about what had happened to my mother. I had so many questions. Exactly how old was my mother when this happened? How did my grandmother respond? Was any action taken against the stepfather? What had happened to the baby? Who else knew about this? I was also shocked that she had managed to hide it from us for so many years. I thought of the kind, caring, soft-spoken mother I had always known. How could such a terrible thing have happened to her?

Part of me wanted to talk to her right away. The other part wanted to protect her from having to dig up old memories. I knew that I was touching upon the most painful experiences of her life. I was torn— should I ask her my questions or should I let the ghosts of her past stay hidden away? To what extent was my curiosity in service of her highest good, and to what extent was it in service of my own? I asked my heart to guide me and tell me what to do.

While I waited for its answer, I continued to pray, sing, and will it to stay open, despite the pain of knowing this truth about my mother.

At work, I was utterly preoccupied with the events from sixty-eight years ago. At home, I didn't know what to say. The one person I wanted to speak with right away was Diana. She had responded immediately to my email about why I was afraid of the dark and we had scheduled time to meet. I kept telling myself that I just had to hold myself together until my appointment with Diana.

Diana sat in her straight-backed chair as always. Spencer seemed slightly agitated, which was unusual, but he calmed down after our greeting. Perhaps I calmed down, too, but only somewhat; I was bursting to tell her what I had discovered.

As I relayed what my brother had told me at my mother's birthday party, Diana listened intently. She took in everything, showing compassion and empathy for my mother. I became emotional as I told her the story. I shared my deep sadness for my mother, as well as my deep admiration at the woman she had become, despite all that she suffered. She worked hard to give us a good, loving, and safe childhood, never revealing that at one point, her own childhood had been a complete nightmare.

I was glad I had waited to speak to Diana first; she was the perfect person with whom to share something so intimate and painful. I told her how I thought this related to my fear of the dark, finally explaining that one of the things I was most afraid of was sexual assault. It was difficult to speak the words aloud—I had never shared them with anyone before—yet now they had context. When I got to the most difficult truths, Spencer shifted and sighed, but he quickly fell back asleep. It felt good to finally confess the truth about my fear—my worst-case-scenario scene seemed much more valid in the light of what had happened to my mother.

Again, Diana listened with patience and rapt attention.

I concluded by telling her, "I understand that, somehow, my mother passed her memories on to me."

As Diana listened, I could feel her sorrow and her compassion. And in that space, I realized I had something else to tell her—the realization about my soul's purpose that had come to me quite a few weeks earlier. I had not been ready until that moment, but I was so open from processing and sharing what I had learned about my mother that I felt comfortable enough to share my knowledge of my purpose without feeling judged. So I told Diana what my soul's purpose is, how the download had arrived, and how I had spent several sessions sitting on the information without telling her.

In contrast to what I had shared earlier, it seemed less consequential to me—but she didn't take it as such. To the contrary, Diana reacted strongly. She seemed almost frustrated that I had not shared it before.

"Why didn't you tell me?" she asked. "Why didn't you tell me when you first found out?"

As she spoke, she turned away from me; I could feel her energy withdraw.

I don't know how to answer that question even today. There is something deeply challenging about knowing why we're here; it's almost easier *not* to know, because then we have no responsibility. Some part of me was afraid to say it. Some part of me was afraid of what it would mean.

To this day, I am still struck by the massive responsibility that comes with knowing my purpose. It isn't really about the fear of taking action;

it's more about my deep-seated doubt about whether I'll be able to do it. Of course, on one level, I know that I just have to get out of the way so the Creator can do the work. Yet I still struggle with whether I'm capable enough to do what I came here to do.

I didn't have the words to explain this understanding to her at the time, so I remained silent.

Perhaps because of my emotional state, perhaps because of the delicacy surrounding what I had shared about my mother, Diana just stared at me in silence for a few moments. I could see that she was trying to work something out within herself. Then, the frustration left her eyes. She had let it go. She didn't make a story, she didn't let herself move beyond her initial frustration and into anger; she processed it, and released it.

At her suggestion, we moved to the healing table. Diana put on the classical guitar music that I loved so much. As she worked on me, I allowed the emotion to pass out of my body, leaving behind only light.

The next day, I had an appointment to speak with John Newton. The appointment was originally intended to address the fear in my life, but now I had a reason for that fear. Stronger still, it was an ancestral reason.

John works with blocks in his clients' bodies, some of which stem from their own lives and some of which have been left behind by their ancestors. As John describes it, he works on resolving the past that lives in our bodies. When I was first exposed to John's work, I didn't understand what he was doing at all, but his gift was undeniable. During his interview session with Marci and Debra on Your Year of Miracles, other women in the program raised their hands to ask for help with specific issues. One said her knee hurt; another had high anxiety. "Okay," John would answer, "hold on a minute." Then he would sit there in silence with dozens of women listening on the other end of the line until the woman who had raised her hand explained incredulously that her pain had subsided. Whatever he was doing, it had a strong and immediate effect; although I didn't understand what was happening during that first virtual meeting, I believed in it.

Months later, John's name came into my sphere again through casual conversation and I decided to look more closely into his work. I learned that first, he asks an individual to select an unwanted emotion or condition and identify the sensation associated with it. Then he asks the individual whether a memory from the past arose—either from early childhood, as far back as the womb, or even from a past life. Once it did, he would seek out what he called the "key phrase," the statement that the individual affirmed to herself when the memory reached its apex of intensity. Then he would tailor his forgiveness prayer to release the energetic blocks from the individual and, theoretically, others along their family line.

The work with early memories was not new to me. Diana and I had been doing similar work for some time. But as we searched in vain for the source of my fear in my current life's history, and as my past-life regression work failed to reveal it, I had begun to wonder whether the answers lay in my ancestors' histories, not my own.

Scientists believe that females are born with up to two million of their reproductive eggs at birth. Therefore, the egg that contributed to my DNA may have been inside my mother her whole life. Maybe, I was actually there with my mother when she was raped and my very cells remembered the trauma.

A few weeks before I found out the truth about my mother's past, I had seen that John was doing a group session in my local area and that individual appointments were available. I signed up for the group clearing and an individual session. I didn't know when I signed up that his visit would fall at such an important time. Who can rationalize these sorts of synchronicities, these apparent coincidences that are so much more than that? Who can explain the sort of intuitive knowing that would cause me to sign up for an appointment with John Newton the very week I was to find out the truth about the ancestral roots of what plagued me? Was this just a coincidence or was it divine orchestration?

The night before my session with John, I recited his forgiveness prayer. John used the prayer for everything, even things that I felt went far beyond forgiveness, shifting it slightly each time to work with the individual's specific blockages.

Infinite Creator, All That You Are: For me, all my family members, all our relationships, all our ancestors and all their relationships through all time, through all our lives …

For all hurts and wrongs: Physical, mental, emotional, spiritual, sexual and financial through thought, word or deed: Please help us all forgive each other, forgive ourselves, forgive all people and all people forgive us, completely and totally. Please and thank you.

For all suicide, incest, murder, rape, abortion and infidelity through thought, word or deed: Please help us all forgive each other, forgive ourselves, forgive all people and all people forgive us, completely and totally. Please and thank you.

For all times we abandoned or were abandoned; withheld love or had love withheld; weren't nurtured, loved and supported and times we didn't nurture love or support others: Infinite Creator, please help us all forgive, be forgiven and all forgive ourselves, completely and totally. Please and thank you.

Please Infinite Creator, for the highest good: Lift out all weight, pain, burden, sin, death, debt, negativity and limitation of all kind; transform it into your love, and let your love flow back into us, filling and giving us all complete peace, now and forever. Please and thank you. Please and thank you. Please and thank you.

Please help us love and bless each other; love and bless ourselves. Be at peace with each other and at peace with ourselves, now and forever. Please and thank you.

The following morning, I sat opposite John in the small room he used for his private sessions. It was the first time I had met him in person. His eyes drew me in as Diana's had so many times before. He asked me what I was there to address.

My own answer surprised me as my lips formed the single word, "forgiveness."

I came to my senses and immediately retracted my statement. Where had it come from? I had no one to forgive, I told him. "Please ignore what I just said, because I came here to work on my fear of the dark."

John looked at me strangely. "Your fear of the dark," he repeated. "Not forgiveness."

"Right," I answered. "That's right."

He nodded his acceptance. And then he did something I knew was coming, because it's part of his practice. He asked whether I wanted to know where my fear of the dark had come from. Like with the haric healing, I had to give my permission for such deep work to begin.

"I guess so," I said.

"Are you sure?" he asked.

"Yes, I'm sure."

John began. "Where in your body do you feel this fear?"

I heard myself respond clearly, "In my chest." I paused for a moment, then went on. "It's a heaviness, almost like I can't breathe."

"On a scale of one to ten, how intense is it?"

"Eight," I answered.

"Okay. Breathe normally into the sensation and notice the memory or image that comes to you," he said.

I closed my eyes and felt into the sensation as an old scene replayed in my mind. I was lying in my bed as a little girl. Spirits swarmed around me as I recited the Lord's Prayer. In the hope that they would go away, I prayed repeatedly:

Our Father who art in heaven, hallowed be thy name.

Thy kingdom come.

Thy will be done, on earth as it is in heaven.

Give us this day our daily bread;

and forgive us our trespasses,

as we forgive those who trespass against us;

and lead us not into temptation, but deliver us from evil.

I watched myself recite the prayer, over and over again, as I recounted the scene to John.

"What doesn't feel good about this memory?" he asked.

I tried to explain to John why I was so deeply afraid. I could sense spirits all around me and I didn't know whether they were there to harm me or perhaps even to assault me. That made me deeply uneasy.

"In the middle of that experience, what are you saying to yourself?" he asked.

My lips began to quiver and I heard my own voice answer as if moved by something other than myself. "Why are you here?" my voice whispered softly.

John then asked me to take three slow breaths as I felt into the words *Why are you here?* He closed his eyes and I knew he was silently offering ancestral clearings using forgiveness to unravel the charge the old memory carried. I tried to stay with the slow breaths as the words *Why are you here?* echoed throughout my body.

As the energy in the room stopped, I imagined John arriving at the final "Please and thank you."

He then asked, "Noticing the sensation—is it bigger, smaller, or different?"

I told him that the heaviness in my chest felt lighter, but that an intense heat was rising throughout my body. He explained that this was the alchemy taking place. We sat in silence as I felt the heat move through me.

I recounted our session in my mind. The issue I brought, *fear of the dark*; the memory of feeling and sensing spirits all around me; the key phrase, *Why are you here?*

The whole process left me slightly overheated and perplexed. I had said the forgiveness prayer so many times, yet with John there, I knew that something had happened that had never happened before. I didn't know *what*, exactly, but the heaviness in my chest had lifted and I felt lighter.

As our individual session ended, John's eyes sparkled as he said, "Everything will unfold for you in perfect timing."

Several hours later, the group clearing began. In amazement, I watched as John worked with person after person. I still could not make sense of our session together or what had happened during it.

As I sat there observing the others, something began to stir in me. Again, I heard the sound of things snapping into place, just like the lock that had clicked when I met Diana, but on a smaller scale and in rapid-fire succession. This wasn't just one click; it was a series, as if *everything* were coming together.

Then, I sensed a vision. It wasn't in front of my eyes; instead, it was just there, all around me and ever-present. I felt my mother lying in bed as a child. She lay in the dark, just as I had lain in the dark so many times in my own memory. A man entered the room. It was a man she knew; it was a man she *trusted*; her mother's partner.

"Why are you here?" she asked.

He didn't answer.

The memory swirled away because what happened next was unthinkable. I knew how the story went; I didn't need to relive the details. It had been banished from both my mother's memory and my own.

After the workshop with John, I began to research a term I had heard in recent months but had never truly understood, *epigenetics*. John had referenced it during the group clearing.

Ever since Charles Darwin had published *On the Origin of Species* in 1859, scientists had begun to accept the idea that natural selection affects which aspects of a parent will be passed down to their offspring. This understanding grew and developed until it became generally accepted that this was done through some sort of code—a code that James Watson and Francis Crick famously identified in 1953 as the *double helix*. As we now understand, DNA arranges itself into a sort of spiral-shaped ladder that provides the structure for who and what each one of us becomes.

But some things were still unexplained by this theory. It seemed that certain learned attributes—things that, ostensibly, were *not* part of a person's particular DNA—were being passed down as well. Scientists could not understand this; their understanding of DNA structure didn't support it, yet it seemed to be true. Many ancient cultures had allegories about spirals, serpents, and ladders, all of which now lined up with the science. But they also talked about things like ancestral healing, which includes both our ancestors' support of our current healing and the idea that our healing in the here and now somehow also heals our forebearers, even though they have passed on. These things were still seen as contrary to science; they were almost fantastical.

Then, in the early 2000s, scientists began to understand that the way a gene expresses is nearly as important as the gene itself—and that, unlike a person's genes, the expression of a gene can be modified through the experiences a person lives out. Genes can be turned "on" and "off." And like the DNA itself, this flip from "on" to "off" (or vice versa) can be passed down to future generations.

I took this to mean that my mother's trauma could be encoded on me. It wasn't just the makeup of her DNA that she had passed down to me; it was the expression of it, as well. Experiences, stories, and traumas had encoded on her body and then, years later, onto my own.

I was living, experiencing, and fearing the very things she had lived, experienced, and feared, because her experiences had affected the very DNA she passed down to me.

This scientific explanation lined up perfectly with John's work. It suggested that my fear of the dark and of sexual assault *did* have a root—but it wasn't from my own lifetime or even from a past life my soul once lived. The root couldn't be found in my own soul's story at all. It could be found in my mother's. But if I could heal it in me, I could keep it from being passed down the line. And perhaps healing it in me could also help heal it in her.

I understood all of this intellectually, but there was still a giant revelation to come. This download would encode the meaning of epigenetics and ancestral healing on my heart forever.

The next morning, I was going through my regular routine when the download arrived. I had just stepped into the shower and was standing under the hot water. My husband was in London on a business trip and I was all alone. Suddenly, I sensed a fog drifting into my consciousness. It felt heavy and, as it got closer, its weight increased. Then, in an instant, it surrounded me. It came in like a memory, or a memory of a memory: The entire, awful scene. The horror of what had happened to my mother the night she was raped.

As the solidity of the scene began to dissipate, I felt the presence of a soul and immediately realized it belonged to my mother's stepfather. The one who had assaulted her. And just as suddenly, I realized that I recognized the soul. It was a soul I had grown to love and trust.

I tried to dismiss it as just a thought. How could Diana share a soul with my mother's rapist? Nonsense.

But my body nagged at me. The sensation of *truth* wouldn't go away. This was the kind of knowing that could not be denied. My whole body was filled with emotion. Somehow, some way, this inconceivable, illogical thing was true. *He is Diana. Diana is him. They are one and the same.*

I stepped out of the shower as I began to cry. Wrapping myself in a towel, I stumbled toward my bed with water still dripping from my legs and hair. I crawled under the covers. The knowing was in every cell now; my very DNA recognized it as true. I began to wail into my pillow, my body racked with heaving sobs. As I was hit by wave after wave of overwhelming sensations, I found I could barely breathe.

"Everything will unfold for you in perfect timing," John had said. I remembered how his eyes had sparkled as he said it. "It's right in front of you."

There it was, right in front of me, every bit of it unfolding. I knew the truth of what happened. I knew it was horrible. I knew it was one of the worst things a human could do to another human. In the shock of it, begging the Creator for help was the only thing I could manage to do. I could have felt betrayal, anger, or even fear—but I didn't. Instead of making a story about it, I felt an entire array of sensations moving through me.

Even without a story, it was still overwhelming. My pillow wet with the tears pouring from my eyes and the water still clinging to my hair, I fell into a fitful sleep.

All that day, I barely left my bedroom. I was a total wreck. I would cry, try to get up, start crying again, and crawl back into bed. I wandered around my house in pajamas and slippers, grateful that my husband couldn't see me like that. But each time, I would quickly return to the bedroom. Despite my fears, it was still the place I felt safest. I wanted to reach out to someone—anyone—who might understand.

Most of what I felt didn't come with words. If someone had asked me, "What's wrong?" I don't know that I could have explained it. It's hard to explain even now. After spending months opening my heart, it had become open enough to let everything in, and now everything *was* in. Everything.

At some point in the afternoon, my husband called from London. He often did this when he traveled to say goodnight before he went to sleep. I kept my voice steady as best I could. It was maybe a one-minute phone call, yet I was grateful to hear his voice; it was a comfort to me, even though I couldn't tell him what was happening.

Throughout the rest of the afternoon, waves of emotion continued to arrive. They would hit me and knock me to the ground where I sobbed uncontrollably. Then I would come up for air, gasping, pulling in as much life as I could before I was knocked down again. I remembered myself at the seashore with my older brother and sister when we were children. They stood strong and held my hands while my tiny body was knocked down by wave after wave.

Now, there was no one to hold my hand—no one who might understand. The only one was Diana. She was the one person I could tell. She was also the one person I *couldn't* tell.

At one point in the evening, I saw a piece of paper sitting on my nightstand. It was John's forgiveness prayer. I began reciting it over and over, just as I had recited the Lord's Prayer as a child. As each wave of emotion came, my words would be drowned by tears, but as soon as I came up for air I would keep going where I had left off before. "Please and thank you," I repeated, "please and thank you." I knew that it would be easy to create a story about the emotional waves hitting me, and I knew how deeply damaging creating a story about them would be. As I said John's prayer, I connected with the highest part of me, the one who knows that there are no stories to create. I willed myself to stay present with my emotions instead of labeling them. "Please and thank you. Please and thank you."

As the crisis from this realization started to pass and I began to feel functional again, a new knowing formed within me. There, in slippers in my bedroom, I knew that I had to tell Diana what I had discovered. There was something so profound in it, almost miraculous; I was struck by the idea that her soul had come into my life to heal this through me, a generation down the family line. I needed to tell her that she played an important role in the middle of this incredible healing miracle—both the being she was now, today, known as Diana, and the being she had once been. I was bound to tell her about her own past life and the role she had played in my family's history.

Doing this would risk everything. It would risk the bond we had built. It would risk her ability to comfortably work with me again in a professional capacity. And it would risk hurting her. Was she even ready to hear it? Just as I feared hurting my mother by bringing up the ghosts of her past, I was worried about how Diana would take this new development. I was far less afraid that she wouldn't believe me than I was afraid that she would be devastated to learn of the role she had played in my family's history.

I had to tell her. "Dear Diana," I wrote. "Can I see you tomorrow? It's an emergency."

She responded immediately and I arranged to come after work. Somehow, I was going to make it through a day at the office; somehow, I was going to hold my heart open, keep myself from creating stories, and feel everything, all while being surrounded by colleagues and holding it together. And then, when the day was done, I would tell Diana.

Somehow.

Part Two Integration

Reflections

The work I did over the months preceding my revelation was essential, because it was only when the blocks began to dissolve that I could truly feel. I realized that emotions come with physiological sensations and it is through these sensations that they are released. In fact, without a story, sensations are all that emotions really are. We don't need to label them as anything. It isn't through thinking about our emotions, rationalizing them, or understanding them that we move through them—this was a false understanding that I'd had for a long time. To the contrary, emotions move through us. And they need space to do that. They need to not be blocked by our thoughts, our stories, or the ways we hang onto our past.

We dissolve the blocks and create that space by opening our hearts. Then, we work to keep them open as the emotions flow through. When we label our emotions, events, and stories, they fall into two categories: love and fear. Fear is just a negative or contracted story. So when we drop the fear, only love remains. Love is the universal truth; it is who we are.

I'm not saying this process is always easy, or that I'm able to do it all the time, even today. Yet the effects can be life-changing. It was only by having an open heart and allowing the Creator in that I could understand Diana's role in my family's history.

As I sat with the revelation of Diana's role in my mother's story, John Newton's prayer helped me immensely. I could have created a story at any moment. I could have felt betrayal or even fear. I could have allowed these contracted energies to consume me. But I didn't. Instead, I allowed my heart to expand so the healing could occur. So instead of letting my feelings stagnate, I occupied my mind with the prayer and let the emotions pass without labels.

Even without labels, I can say that the day I spent in bed was not pleasant; it was hard and it pushed me to my very edge. It took work to not create a story. I found myself wishing it would last only ninety seconds (the time it takes to feel an emotion), but I realized that sometimes, processing takes longer than that. If we can keep ourselves from succumbing to judgment during that time, if we can keep our hearts open, it doesn't make it easy; it just makes it easier.

The heart wants to open; we just don't always know how to let it. But I was prepared to do this, in part, because I had been putting these lessons into practice in very practical ways. Working with the guitar was one of them. Playing the guitar forced me to be entirely present; I would quite literally lose track of my mind in the bodily experience, just feeling the sensations move through me. I later learned that classical music can open up our chakras and allow us to be more present in our bodies. With the body of the guitar pressed against my heart space, the vibrations shook my heart chakra open while simultaneously giving my mind a singular point of focus and allowing me to express emotions that had lain dormant for years. Singing, even though I was off-key, was also an important practice. It put me back in my body and let me detach from my mind.

Physical activity is another great way to make this happen. When my kids were young, our whole family trained in martial arts. My years getting beaten and bruised by other students as we sparred were deeply healing for me. Not only did I learn to defend myself—something I had not known how to do as a child—but because it required me to be fully present, I began to have experiences that brought me out of my head and back into my body. I felt incredibly alive.

Feeling gratitude and love are also both instrumental in this process. When we feel gratitude, we create chemical changes in our brain that cause us to seek out more causes for gratitude. In other words, we rewire ourselves for happiness. Love works the same way. Envisioning my loved ones' faces, one by one, there on Diana's table, forced me into a loving space. As each image flashed before my eyes, my heart would begin to flood with love, joy, and gratitude. That's because when we picture or imagine the people and places we love, we reawaken the love within us, which is our true, eternal self. We remember who we really are.

By using these tools, my heart opened and gave my mind something to do—block the next hit while sparring, read the notes of the sheet music, remember the lyrics of what I was singing, count the things for which I am grateful, visualize the faces of the people I love—so it could be busy enough to stay quiet. Then I let the heart do its work. In this way, the mind was in service of the heart; the heart became my driving force.

When we open our hearts, there is truly only love inside; this is what I found in mine. I now see that forgiveness, gratitude, and compassion are all different forms of love. Forgiveness is a gift we give ourselves. It's an act of self-love. It means to forego; it means to release. It's not dependent on the other person's actions, and it's not for the other person. Instead, true forgiveness allows us to release the contracted, negative energies and stories so that we can move forward. It allows us to release the past.

Since I had not created a story about what Diana's soul had done in a previous incarnation, I was able to see it from this space of love. I could see that she and I had reconnected in this lifetime to heal what had happened in another. Her soul, seeking redemption, had found my mother's wound living in me. The ancestral wound within me had found her to provide the healing her soul needed to receive. She was given the chance to heal her action, and through our work together, she was healing both me and my mother. Unsurprisingly, the wound I carried from my mother had originally manifested on my uterus, a representation of sexuality, creativity, and the very violation that my mother had suffered as a child. And things had gone exactly as the Creator had meant for them to go; we had found each other, giving us a chance for a healing that was sixty-eight years in the making. Everything was divinely orchestrated.

I could also see that Diana herself was deeply instrumental in helping me process my mother's history and Diana's role in it. During the many hours we spent in her office, she created a safe space for me to embrace who I truly am. This made it safe for me to be fully present in my body without the fear of judgement or labels. She encouraged this throughout our time together. This allowed me to drop the stories I had about myself: That I was different, that I couldn't use my voice, and that I was incomplete somehow. By giving me the space I needed to be myself, Diana was subtly preparing me for the work to come—she just didn't know the role she would be playing in it.

Finally, I would be remiss if I didn't give credit to the ones who led me there—who led me both to Diana, through my healing, and into understanding the truth about her tie to my family's history. My guides were there, loving and supporting me through the entire process. I could never have done it alone, and luckily, I didn't have to. As I learned to work with them, I opened myself to receive. I could ask for them to reveal my purpose, for instance, which they did. I could ask to work on forgiveness, as I did in the session with John Newton (surprising even myself!), and right away, I was given an opportunity to understand forgiveness as I had never done before.

After living most of my life believing I was so unique and different that I was utterly alone in the world, I came to understand that our isolation is an illusion. We have not been abandoned; we are surrounded by infinite love and support. We are never alone.

Exercises

These exercises accompanied me through the journey I described in part two of this book, so I present them here to you. They helped me to open my heart and ask for what I truly desired.

I can point to a few key things I began doing in my daily life that helped me to truly feel my emotions and process them simply as sensations without labels. These were essential elements in my process.

Sing, and Let Your Spirit Find Its Voice

Diana recommended that I sing to open up my throat chakra. I found myself singing before our healing sessions so that I could more easily express what I was feeling. But I soon found it had other applications throughout my life. I began singing before important presentations at work. I found that it did in fact open my throat chakra and it also gave me the forward momentum to continue my verbal expression.

I also found that the vibration was not only limited to my throat but it expanded to my chest and actually opened up my other chakras as well. Research has shown that chakra toning can be used as a healing instrument by singing the notes of the musical scale and letting them vibrate through your body. It is a soothing experience that brings peace and alignment to your energy. Beginning with the root chakra and continuing to the crown chakra, you can either sing the solfege name of the note (do, re, mi, fa, sol, la, ti) or the chakra name of the tone (lam, vam, ram, yam, ham, aum, om).

See how singing can create a simple shift in your day:

1. Find songs that are in alignment with the mood you want to create. Remember what it feels like when a song comes on the radio and gives you a boost of energy, joy, and vitality. This is an opportunity for you to consciously choose music that will put you into your desired state.

2. Create your own playlist and sing! Commit to the habit of singing every day.

3. Soon you will find yourself looking forward to this ritual!

You Are Love

The essence of who we are is love. To tap into this universal life force, we must be in vibrational alignment with that force. We don't have to look outside ourselves; we can create it in an instant. A wonderful way to send that feeling toward oneself is through a letter of appreciation. See what happens when you try the following process:

1. Sit down and think about all the different things that you have achieved in your life so far. Think about your favorite moments of joy or the challenges that you have overcome.

2. Then write a letter to yourself about all the different ways that you appreciate who you are—it can be on a beautiful piece of stationery or on a specially chosen card.

3. Shower yourself with love! Write about all of your wonderful qualities: Your smile, your humor, your courage, your compassion, and your service to others. The idea is to shower yourself with all the love, appreciation, and gratitude that you would bestow upon another.

4. When you are done, address the envelope and mail it to yourself. See what it feels like when you receive it in the mail!

The second exercise that works with this point is an adaptation from Dr. Sue Morter's book, *The Energy Codes*. In the chapter devoted to the heart chakra, Dr. Sue talks about tapping directly into the vibration of love by feeling into the experiences that elicit love (it could be picturing a loved one, a place that we love, or even an experience that we are hoping to have). As I lay on the healing table, I would bring person after person that I loved into my mind. In this heightened state of love, my heart chakra began to open. I began to live from a more heart-centered space and I was able to connect with the Universe more easily. I learned that I could quickly recreate that state for myself.

Here is a simple adaptation of the process to create a sense of love and well-being:

1. Close your eyes and take a deep breath in and slowly exhale. A slow breath calms the heart and quiets the mind.

2. As you exhale, imagine all of your fears, doubts, and worries being released.

3. Take another deep breath in and gently exhale.

4. Feel your heart calming.

5. In this calm state, imagine someone or something you love. It can be a person; a pet; or an image, such as a beautiful sunset.

6. Truly feel and connect with that loving emotion. Experience it with all of your senses. What are you doing, seeing, feeling, hearing? Let every cell of your body be immersed in that experience.

7. You can magnify this feeling even further by bringing in another image or memory and feel the love expand.

8. Repeat the practice described above several times until you feel an overwhelming sense of love.

9. Notice how you feel. Memorize the feeling. Then put your hand on your heart and tell yourself that this is for you; this love that you have created is meant for you. This is you!

10. You can also imagine instances of gratitude. Love and gratitude are two of the highest vibrations energetically and you can create them for yourself—they are not dependent on anyone or anything.

While in this heightened state, I've found it useful to create a link to something in this world. The link triggers the memory, which triggers the feeling. For instance, I can gently place my hand on my heart and instantly trigger that feeling of love. You can also make the link by connecting it to a song, a picture, or an object such as a small stone. As you take time each day to imagine and experience this love, you can repeatedly link it to that object or picture. You can then quickly elicit that same feeling instantly by seeing or holding that specific object, such as the small stones that I carry with me to represent my father and my uterus.

In the Asking, You Open Yourself to Receive

Throughout my journey, I've learned that we are never alone—we are surrounded by a loving and supportive Universe. However, we must learn to ask for what we want. It is in the asking that we open ourselves to receiving. Oftentimes, it can feel challenging to discover what we truly want. This exercise is designed to help with that.

It is often in the contrasts of life that we can hear the desires of our hearts. The next time that you are having a challenging time identifying what you truly want, try this exercise:

1. Write down all the things you don't want in your life.

2. Next to each item, write down the opposite statement. This can help point you in the direction of your truest desires. For example, *I often can't find the words to express what I am feeling*. The opposite would be *I easily find the words to confidently express what I am feeling.*

3. Once you have identified your desire, remember to clearly express it in the positive form, as like attracts like. For example, rather than saying, *I want to get out of debt* (a contracted energy), phrase it as, *I am living in financial abundance* (a positive and expansive energy).

4. Express your desire in the present tense as if it were already here. This sends a clear message to the Universe that you are ready to receive your intention. If you phrase it in the future tense (*I will experience financial abundance by next December*, for example), you are clearly stating that you have not yet received your intention and the Universe may continue to delay its arrival.

Another way to hone in on your desires is to pay attention to the feelings they generate. Do these feelings expand or contract your energy? Does it bring you joy? Does it make you smile? Does it make you feel alive? Give yourself permission to truly embrace those positive emotions. Oftentimes, it is not the physical object or possession that we long for but the feelings that it creates. You can try this out for yourself:

1. Set a timer for two minutes and write down everything that you want to be, have, or do. As you are doing this exercise remember that there is no wrong answer. Proceed with full confidence that there is no such thing as failure. If you let go of your fears, what would you dare to do? What would you ask for?

2. Sometimes, the act of just setting the timer helps the most important desires of your heart rise to the top.

3. Next, beside each item, write the feeling that the item will bring you.

In this simple exercise, what you truly desire can be revealed. Is it really the money that you are seeking or the freedom that it brings? Is it the fancy clothes or is it the confidence you feel when you wear them? Or do you simply want to feel successful, worthy, accepted, or part of a community?

Once you have identified your desires, write down the three that make your heart truly expand with joy. I like to limit things to three items because it is a manageable amount that can receive the full strength of my attention. When you are juggling five or six intentions, you can start to feel overwhelmed, so keep it simple.

Now it's time to set up a simple intentions practice:

1. At the start of each day or before you go to bed at night, take a moment to fully feel that the object of your desire is already here.

2. Go beyond the act of visualization. What are all the physical sensations of your manifested desire? What are you seeing, hearing, feeling, and tasting? Engage all of your senses. By activating

your senses, you are creating the vibration that will allow your dreams to be manifested.

3. Repeat the process for your remaining two desires.

Your mind does not know the difference between an imaginary emotion and one that is real. In the same manner, you can create the feelings and sensations that you would be experiencing if the desires of your heart were already fulfilled—feelings of greater joy, peace, and happiness.

Part Three

"You are the light, the love, the infinite power
of all that is, was, and ever will be."

— Judi Miller

Chapter Nine

The Risk

I knew I had to speak with Diana. I knew exactly what I wanted to convey. I just had no idea how to say it.

I've always been pretty logical. I spent my early life planning out most of my conversations, and certainly the conversations that I anticipated would be difficult. As time went on, I learned that I no longer had to try and always control the outcome. I trusted the Universe to unfold everything perfectly, instead of inserting my will into it. This helped me stay present in the moment, surrendering to whatever was meant to be.

This process took some time. When I began to meet with Diana, I had progressed significantly and was able to be more present. But I still tried to make a mental list of important things to bring up during our time together. And surprisingly, these lists just disappeared during our sessions. Our conversations gave me exactly what I needed—not *despite*, but *because* of the fact that I wasn't trying to control everything. The higher version of myself that comes from the heart, not the mind, took over and directed the conversation exactly as the Creator intended.

Yet as I drove to our session that day, I was worried that she wouldn't believe me, or worse—that she would, and it would hurt her terribly. Still, I couldn't think of what to say. My mind was completely frozen. I would like to say there was some higher wisdom to it and that I yielded and surrendered to it. But in truth, I was so frozen that I had no other option; the only thing I *could* do was let my heart lead me through the conversation. I tried to remind myself that throughout the whole experience, I had felt guided and I hoped desperately that when it came to having the conversation, I would be guided again.

That's how I ended up in my car, driving to see Diana, listening to "Perfect," knowing I was going to have a very serious conversation with her and having no plan whatsoever for executing it. I sat hesitantly in front of her house. Inside, she was awaiting my arrival. Both she and Spencer would be happy to see me, as they usually were.

I looked down at the birthday gift sitting on the passenger seat beside me—a wooden carving depicting a crane—and I hoped it would be as meaningful to her as it was to me. I had pulled it from my desk drawer, where I kept small things from my travels around the world that I liked but never seemed to have a place to put at home. I had brought it back from Japan before Diana and I met. The Japanese crane represents good fortune and longevity, both gifts that I would have given her, if I could.

I had only just found out it was Diana's birthday. A few hours earlier, after scheduling the appointment, I had asked for a sign to show me that the revelation I had experienced over the weekend was true. It felt true in my heart, but my head doubted the plausibility that she and my mother's stepfather shared a soul. I got it in my head that, if this were true, she would have to be younger than me—she would have to have been born *after* me, with some sort of agreement to heal me. At the time, this was what my mind was doing in search of logic it could understand. I did a quick google search and saw something unexpected: It was her birthday *that very day,* as I sat there searching for it. It was her birthday *on the very day we were scheduled to meet.*

I sat, staring at the computer screen. I looked back to the birthdate next to her name on the records website. I looked at the date in the lower right corner of my screen. The month and day were exactly the same. I was searching for Diana's birthday *on* her birthday. I was dumbfounded. How could this be just a coincidence?

As I've processed everything that happened, I've thought a lot about coincidences. I believe that the major events in our lives are divinely orchestrated, set up for us, holding a specific purpose or reason. And that coincidences are a way for the Creator to remind us that we are never alone, and that we're always loved.

But a coincidence like this went far beyond a sign that we are never alone. To me, the coincidence around Diana's birthday felt like confirmation that my revelation was true: Diana and my mother's stepfather somehow shared a soul. I asked for a sign, and this was a *direct message* from the Universe.

The fact that the sign came in the form of a birthday had additional significance. It marked a rebirth for both of us. In the wake of everything that transpired, I had become someone new. The person I had been before I met Diana could never have handled the revelation about her past life without feeling betrayal, anger, or resentment. I was changed.

Yet still, my logical mind argued back at me. "Prove it," my inner skeptic demanded. "Let's see a second sign." I was sure that two signs would surely be enough to quiet the doubt.

So I sat down with my favorite oracle deck, Kyle Gray's *Keepers of the Light*. I asked the Universe to show me whether my revelation was true. My logical mind still wanted to be sure. I shuffled the deck and then slowly drew a card, holding it with my eyes closed for a moment before opening them.

The image showed a Roman goddess with a quiver full of arrows across her back, a headdress of gold leaves set upon her dark brown hair, and the moon shining from her crown chakra. Beneath the image, the words *focused intention* were printed. *Think about what you desire,* the card advised. *Set your sights high. Expect the best possible outcome.* Her eyes pierced my own like the stars in the night sky surrounding her. I didn't even need to look at the name below the image, because I knew the deck well.

The goddess pictured on the card I pulled was *Diana*.

After asking for a sign, I had received one that was unmistakable. Yet still, I had asked for another. The Universe complied by putting the card bearing her name right in my hand.

So, though I didn't have the remotest idea of how to bring it up, I knew that the Creator and the Universe itself were supporting me. I set my sights high and focused my intention on the best possible outcome: First, that Diana would believe me, and second, that sharing my revelation would help us release the trauma, the pain and the burdens of the past so we could all be healed.

In the car, the final bars of "Perfect" played and the stereo cut to silence. I looked toward the window of Diana's office, knowing it was now or never. I pulled open the door handle, got out of my seat, and walked down the path toward her front porch.

Diana was immediately happy to see me. Her enthusiasm was palpable. Spencer was exuberant as usual, and I knelt down to greet him, avoiding Diana's eyes. Would she be hurt by what I had to say? How could I communicate something so grave without affecting her?

I got up and followed Diana into her office. She sat in her straight-backed office chair as I settled into the recliner. Spencer did his customary three turns before finding the perfect spot on his bed. Then he promptly went to sleep.

"Happy birthday," I said, making true eye contact with Diana for the first time.

Her piercing eyes, the eyes of the panther, blinked back at me in surprise. "How did you know it was my birthday?" she asked, seeming pleased by it. "Was it guidance?"

Diana had always believed in me and my guidance. She never doubted me—not the way I sometimes doubted myself.

"Sorta-kinda ..." I answered. I was struggling to figure out how to say what I was going to share with her, because I still had no idea how to do it. Her enthusiasm about seeing me made me even more self-conscious about my utter lack of a plan.

As usual, when I was nervous, my eyes darted down to Spencer for reassurance. He was completely calm, eyes closed, in that half-sleep half-joy state that dogs embody perfectly. For a moment, it flashed into my mind that the relationship I had formed with Diana could change drastically. What if she thought I was imagining things, decided I was totally crazy, and never wanted to see me again? The whole thing seemed far-fetched, logically speaking. Worse, what if I really hurt her? I know that, often, the perpetrator is more hurt by wrongdoing than the victim. Part of me worried that she wouldn't believe me; the other part worried that she would, and that it would devastate her.

My heart told me to speak, so I began. First, I went through the fears I had shared with her—including my fear of sexual assault, which I had confessed to her only a few days before. Then, I reminded her of the story she had once told me about when she and her teacher in a past-life regression workshop both realized that they had shared a lifetime together. I explained the experience allowed them to realize theirs was not a chance encounter; it was their opportunity to heal.

Diana leaned forward and nodded. She remembered.

I repeated what I had told her a few days before, about what happened to my mother when she was a child. Diana looked at me intently as she listened to me retell it.

Then I heard myself saying the words out loud: "Maybe this is *our* opportunity to heal. I can't explain it, Diana, but I think you're him. I think you and my mother's stepfather share a soul. And I think you and I were reborn in this lifetime with the plan to meet so we could heal it."

My words sat, surrounded by silence, and as the eyes of the panther burned back at me, I tried not to cry.

Diana continued listening, completely engaged. I explained everything; everything I had felt over the weekend as the realization sunk in, and how important it was that we had met again in this lifetime. The words spilled from my mouth spontaneously. As they did, the tears increased their threat to do the same. It didn't feel like I was even the one speaking; the voice was mine, but the words were much older than this body. Then, I heard my voice crack as it softly whispered, "I promised to find you."

For a moment, I stopped speaking and let the words hang in the air. I didn't fully know what they meant. They weren't coming from the logical part of me, yet I knew they were true. I *had* promised to find her, somewhere, sometime in the distant past. My soul remembered beyond the confines of Judi and Diana, back to when we had agreed to this story. It was long before this lifetime.

Diana sat forward in her chair, her shoulders pushed toward me and her face grave with concern. Though she had barely said a word, I could see that she believed everything I said. She always had; she had believed me unconditionally, and now was no exception.

I was shocked that she had handled it so well. Though I had spent a lot of energy trying to put logic into it, looking for signs and confirmation that it was true, she just accepted it. It was impressive. We had a strong relationship, and here I was, sharing how her soul had done something so unimaginable to my mother, and she trusted me completely; she held space for all of it.

She didn't balk; she didn't deny it or treat me like I was crazy. And though I could feel her sadness, she didn't seem devastated. Neither of my worst-case scenarios had come true.

Instead, she just believed me. Her quiet acceptance was the best thing that could have happened as she created space for us both to be healed.

Slowly, Diana stood up. "Would you like to do a healing session?" she asked.

I followed her to the healing table.

I had gotten more comfortable on the table. Relaxing into it was still slow, but it was quicker than it had been months before when I had first met Diana. And I was always quite warm. I never asked for a blanket, and she had stopped offering. But that day, she offered, and I accepted. Slowly, I fastened the buttons on my sweater one by one, even though I was warm. I noted this as odd at the time, and in retrospect, I don't fully know why I did it, but maybe I needed some sort of barrier between us. Was I trying to psychologically protect myself from this person I had come to love and trust? With the trajectories of our souls so entangled, I needed to know where she ended and I began.

She began at my feet, as always, grounding me down into the earth. Slowly, chakra by chakra, her hands made their way up the center line of my body. There was such sadness in her touch. I'm hesitant to label emotions these days, but the heaviness was palpable, and it's a heaviness I usually associate with heartbreak and grief—the kind of sadness that sits on your heart. Over the months, her hands had ranged from cold to lukewarm to downright hot. Today, they held a gentleness, almost like a silent knowing that this was goodbye.

Diana arrived at my crown and completed the healing. Then, as she always did, she stood there, waiting until I slowly sat up.

"I felt the divine presence of Jesus today," she said.

"So did I." My lips almost whispered the words.

I was amazed that our experiences were in such perfect alignment.

To me, Jesus is unconditional love, always accepting us without question. He shows us why forgiveness is never necessary, because the Creator never condemns. We both felt his presence that day, reminding us that both of us are—and always have been—loved.

Then, she spoke again. She looked directly at me as she formed the sentence—a simple sentence, but one that has stuck with me since that day.

"Does this mean we're done?"

My answer was simple. I didn't know whether it would be forever. I didn't know what the next minute would be like, let alone the next few weeks or months. But I knew I needed time and space to process it all. So with full love for her in my heart, I told her yes, we were done. I confirmed what I had felt during the hands-on part of the session: That this was our final healing session.

Before leaving, I gave her the birthday gift. She opened it slowly and gazed at it. I explained what it represented and said that I wished both good fortune and longevity for her. I would always wish her well, I said, regardless of the past. In some ways, it didn't matter who she had been; it mattered who she was now. I told her I loved her and thanked her for everything.

She hugged me one last time and I reached down to pat Spencer, who had barely moved the whole session. Then, I went home knowing that my life would be forever changed.

That night, I couldn't fall asleep, so I listened to one of Sonia Choquette's meditations to calm myself.

I find Sonia's meditations deeply moving. I am so focused on her words and engaged in the experience that it feels like I am traveling. Wherever she guides me, I go completely. I traveled with Sonia that night, letting her lead the way, until the meditation completed. And as it ended, I heard the distinct sound of bells.

In an instant, I felt the presence of my grandmother. It had been some twenty years since I had last seen her; she died when my kids were young. Yet there she was. My grandmother, my mother's mother, was with me.

I had heard these same bells a few months before. I was visiting the city where my grandmother had lived and where some family members still live today. I had awoken from a deep sleep to the sound. It was so real that I searched the house for anything that could have made the sound, but there was nothing. Perhaps my grandmother had been visiting me that day, too.

But this time, I knew it was her. The knowing was immediate. I felt her eyes focused on me. They were filled with tears.

Then, she gave me a message. *Tell your mother how sorry I am that I could not protect her. Tell her that she was and always will be loved. Please tell her.* I felt her gaze imploring me to deliver the message.

I let her words permeate my being, knowing that I would act on them; I would do exactly what my grandmother asked. Even though she was dead, there was nothing frightening about her visitation. Her request was directive but gentle. I understood this was part of my role in the healing process.

Still present with my grandmother, I drifted off to a peaceful sleep.

I awoke with a jolt to the sound of crying. Around me, the room was dark, but I was in another room, too; I was back with my mother on the night she was assaulted. The crying grew stronger, and it was not mine. It was the sound of a twelve-year-old girl whose cries had gone unheard. She called out for help, but no one came to rescue her. No one heard. Sixty-eight years later, her soul still cried, begging to finally be heard.

Then, a second cry rose up, wailing in harmony with the sound of my mother's. It was the cry of a soul who had done great harm and regretted it. This second cry pleaded for redemption and the release of the pain that had been passed down through the generations. Together, the two cries formed the voice of our family line and everyone connected to it. Their harmony held all of us—the stepfather, my mother, and me—finally ready to be free of the past. I felt the highest part of myself lean forward and kiss each of the other two souls on the forehead.

"You are loved," I whispered to each of them.

As the vision faded away, I felt the Universe and the Creator smile. We had done our work—what we came here to do. We had freed ourselves and each other. We had freed the whole family from this pain and suffering. We were finally healed.

After that night, I knew I had to speak with my mother. She needed to hear the message my grandmother had sent, no matter how painful it would be to relive the events of the past. But first I had to tell her that I knew what had happened. As far as I was aware, very few people knew of the events that had taken place sixty-eight years before.

I wanted her to understand that she wasn't alone; not when it happened, and not now. None of us is. Each of us is always accompanied by the Creator, our ancestors, and our guides. And as I now understand, I was there too, because the cells that would one day become me accompanied the whole process. In every action we take, we act for many generations. Our pain and our healing are family events.

That meant whatever was happening with me and Diana was also a part of the healing process. I knew that what I said might have hurt her; as the days following my revelation unfolded, she might feel a heaviness and responsibility for having done something so unimaginable. I didn't want to cause her pain. I cared for Diana and I worried that she was hurt.

In the days I had spent in bed feeling the weight of this revelation, asking for help and guidance was the only thing I held to. Now, I considered the possibility that Diana was in the same situation, needing support as she let the emotions move through her. And once I spoke with my mother, the same would be true for her, too; it would force her to enter into the painful memories she had worked so hard to forget.

I knew that by talking about it, I was bringing the pain to the surface. But if I could impart just one thing upon my mother, and on Diana, it would be this: *Even in our most painful moments, we are never alone, never abandoned, and always loved.*

Chapter Ten

My Mother's Story

I've always struggled to express myself. Speaking up doesn't come easily for me. Even when I know what to say, my throat tightens up and I become paralyzed with fear. I developed a habit of keeping my mouth shut, avoiding speaking about myself and my experiences so I would never have to worry about being judged or hurt. It naturally feels safer to not speak.

I've always suspected that I got this trait from my mother. She's never found it easy to speak up for herself or share what she's feeling. Doing the hard work, showing up day after day, taking care of everyone else—these things come naturally to her. But saying what she feels simply doesn't.

We sat at her kitchen table, just as my brother and I had sat at my kitchen table a few days before. My mother still has the same dining set she had when I was a child. The round, antique tabletop holds so much of our family's history, crossing state lines with us multiple times in my childhood. Beneath me, the wooden seat was hard and I felt the rounded chair back almost wrapped around me. When I was quite young, I used to imagine that these chairs held me as I sat in them.

Today, I needed that support.

My mother was smiling up at me. She looked small, held in a chair of her own. She used to be as tall as me, but she has shrunk in recent years. This was one of the only things that betrayed her true age; though she had just turned eighty, she could pass for at least a decade younger. I studied the fine lines in her face. There is little that resembles me in there; I look much more like my father, and people have always told me as much. I got nearly all of my features from him. But I got one feature from my mother, which she displayed that day in her warm smile: A set of perfectly even dimples.

I smiled back, feeling the connection between us. Then, I gingerly began to ask questions about her past.

I started by asking about her parents' divorce, which I quickly learned had not actually taken place until she was a teenager. My grandparents were entrepreneurs in Trinidad, and in the months leading up to their split, they had fallen on hard times. They had not been wealthy, and they had eight small children to raise. My grandmother's situation was dire in the eyes of her family, friends, and neighbors, and adding a divorce into the mix would have only complicated things. So she didn't file for divorce right away. Even after my grandfather was long gone, my grandmother remained married to him in the legal sense for several years.

"It was difficult to divorce then," my mother concluded.

After my grandfather left the family, the two oldest siblings took on parental roles, raising the rest while my grandmother worked outside the home. Aunt Maggy and Uncle Alfred cooked, cleaned, and played with the younger children, including my mother, who was fourth in line. Uncle Alfred always liked to take care of everyone, a trait that continued into his adult life. My favorite memories of him are set at the large family gatherings he used to host, serving up Trinidadian food bursting with Chinese and Caribbean flavors while the Calypso music pulled me in, beckoning me into the warm and joyful memories of their childhood. I have loving memories of Aunt Maggy, too. The oldest of the eight siblings, she took the motherly role, strict and protective. But I also remember the fear that walked alongside her, and how she used to check under the beds and in the closets upon returning home, looking for someone who might try to hurt us. My mother told us many stories of Aunt Maggy's and Uncle Alfred's protectiveness, including how they would speak up for her as a child because she was so soft-spoken.

Money was tight, but the family was tighter; they managed to create a life for themselves, tightly bonded together by their love. They worked hard and did their best to protect each other. Throughout my life, my mother spoke fondly of her childhood. She never talked about what they lacked; she talked about all they had, and all they made of it.

It was hard to go further in my questioning. I was torn. Although I felt as though I had to know the truth, I also didn't want to hurt her. Perhaps she had left her childhood abuse there, in Trinidad. Why bring it back?

Yet I knew what I had to do, what my grandmother had guided me to say. Despite my hesitation, I kept asking questions.

"Did Granny ever have another husband or a partner?" My mother didn't reply; at first, she didn't seem to know what I was getting at. "But wasn't there ... another man ... another man who lived in your house?" I stumbled over the words, feeling the tension rise as I approached the question I really wanted to ask. My mother's demeanor changed. At first, she stiffened, and I could see the wheels turning in her mind as she began to understand. Then her shoulders softened and her eyes grew more distant. She didn't answer.

"Mom? Did another man ever live in your house when you were a girl?"

She snapped back to the present and looked at me. Yet she remained silent. Unsure as to whether she had fully heard me, and slightly unsure as to whether she realized I was asking for a response, I tried one more time. This time, I was more direct. "Did Granny ever remarry or stay with a man who was abusive? To her or to ... you?"

Though my mother was slow to answer in words, her entire body immediately confirmed that it was true. I saw the younger child still living within her, recounting memories of a life lived long ago. Her lips moved as if to speak, but no words came. She tried again, her lips moving, helplessly. Then, finally, she quietly answered me.

"Yes. There was another man."

She described the man who lived in their home, how she had first met him, and how he had stayed on in their lives in the months to come. She painted him as big, strong, and overpowering, and she didn't waver when she said that he raped her. She told me how she was only twelve, but she became pregnant. How her mother discovered it. As the story flowed from her, I felt her heartbreak, her fear, her agony at keeping such a secret for so long. I kept breathing trying to stay present with an open heart.

Then I thought back to the eyes I had seen the night before: The eyes of my grandmother. "Tell your mother how sorry I am that I could not protect her."

As my mother spoke, I knew it wasn't time for me to speak yet. I wanted to give her time to complete her narrative. My mother was in another place, somehow; her eyes eluded me more and more as she traveled back in time and recounted the events. I listened with an open heart, sending her love and compassion. I stopped asking questions and just witnessed her memories pour out.

She told me how my grandmother immediately took her to the home of some extended family members in the countryside, before she started to really show. How after she gave birth, she never saw her firstborn daughter again, though she believed my grandmother had continued to support the family who adopted her for many years. How even her older siblings were silent about her absence and her younger siblings were completely in the dark about why she had left in the first place. How by the time she returned home, the man who raped her was no longer in her home; in fact, she never saw him again.

In many ways, I thought, the story was typical of the time: A young pregnant girl hidden away from society, sent to live with some relation far from home until the baby was born so she and her family would not be scarred by the shame forever.

Some scars certainly last a while, though. I could still see the evidence of my mother's pain. It was like she was looking at the memory from a distance; the pain so real, yet she could not touch it somehow. I felt her fear, regardless of her distance from it. It was palpable, tangible, like a living, breathing thing. As she described this man and what he did to her, I could sense how long she had been afraid of him.

"You know," she said, looking me in the eyes for the first time in many minutes, "with the internet, anyone can find you now."

I'll never know exactly what she meant by this statement, because by the time I asked who might try to find her, her eyes had that faraway look once more. Together, we sat quietly. I continued to focus on sending her love.

In the silence that followed, my mother and I sat with the grief of this impossible truth. Perhaps an entire lifetime passed as we sat quietly at the worn kitchen table; or, perhaps it was mere minutes. Then, it faded away.

I thought again of my grandmother's message: "Tell her. Tell her that she was and always will be loved."

So I did.

Taking a breath, I felt the words come directly from my heart. I told her that I knew my grandmother had wanted to protect her and was heartbroken that she couldn't do so. I told her that Granny had visited me and told me so. I know my mother heard me, but as I spoke, I felt her retreat to whatever space in the past held her. She was no longer with me; again, she was far away.

As she drifted, I held the space and continued to send her love. I also thought about how unimaginable it seemed. How could my mother have gone through such a horrific thing and still turn out the way she did?

My mother is the type of person that everyone likes. Though she's quiet, people think of her fondly. One summer in college, I went to work with her at her office. I was lucky to get a summer job, but I was even luckier to see her in action. For the first time, I saw my mother in a different light; she wasn't just my mother, she was her own, independent person. Everyone in the office knew her and liked her. They gravitated toward her naturally; they wanted to do things for her. It was remarkable to see her the way the rest of the world saw her.

In our family, she's well-loved, too. I remembered joking with my own daughter one day. I had done something nice for her, and I said, facetiously, "I'm the nicest person you'll ever meet!"

She corrected me immediately: "No, you're not. Grandma is certainly the nicest person I'll ever meet!" And of course, she was right. My mother was as loving to us when we were children as she was as a grandmother. My mother was, is, and has always been an incredible person.

I marveled at that. How could that be true when her own childhood was so scarred?

Sitting at her kitchen table as she wandered through her own memories, I was struck by the thought that if I had gone through something similar, I don't think I would have handled it as well—and especially if I'd had to keep it a secret all that time. Her ability to process such deep trauma amazed me. Somehow, she had found a way. I thought about the challenge I had processed myself that very weekend, realizing that my mother's rapist and my own healer shared a soul. I thought back to how I had handled it: By asking for help and refusing to make a story. Perhaps my mother had processed these events so effectively because she rarely made stories about things. She and my father would occasionally get upset about things, but in general, they didn't try to control and label everything.

As our conversation closed, she seemed more present and coherent, but she also seemed tired. I thanked her for telling me her story and hugged her close. It felt as though we had just opened a door that had not yet closed.

I managed to hold the tears in until I left her house. Then I got into my car and sobbed most of the way home.

I went back to see my mother a few weeks later. We're close, and I see her frequently, but both she and I knew why I was there. We sat at the kitchen table again, the rounded chair backs hugging us and keeping us secure. For a second time, we traveled back in time to her childhood in Trinidad.

This time, my mother led the way. She spoke about her shock when she returned home after giving birth and how even Aunt Maggy and Uncle Alfred, then in their late teens, seemed oblivious to what had gone on. There was now a secret separating them; a shameful, unspeakable thing that she now had to hide.

Did they know what had happened to her? Did they know who had done it? Did they know about the baby, where she went, what became of her? If so, they never let on. The whole family just continued as if everything were normal. Perhaps they did this to protect my mother. Perhaps they wanted to help her move on. I can't help but think she must have been lonely in the silence.

Perhaps in the silence, she was also protecting herself and all of us from the difficult feelings that came along with it. The last person she told—likely the only person she told, after my grandmother—was my father. She was nineteen and they were about to get married. My mother loved my father dearly and, as she explained it, she didn't want there to be any secrets between them. So she told him everything, and he listened.

To my knowledge, he didn't tell anyone else until he was nearing his own death. The months leading up to my father's passing marked a painful time for our whole family, one that changed each of us deeply. In his final days, perhaps in some combination of deathbed confession and dementia, my father told my brother what my mother had told him. And years later, at my mother's eightieth birthday party, my brother told me.

My mother confessed that she was greatly relieved to have the opportunity to talk about these events. It didn't change the past, but it did change the weight of the secret. We sat together, my mother and I, the biggest secret of her life sitting on the kitchen table between us.

I slowly and hesitantly shared the fears I had kept secret for so long; my fear of the dark and being sexually assaulted. I explained to my mother how I would lie awake each night reciting the Lord's Prayer until I would fall asleep exhausted. I saw the tears well up in her eyes and felt the heaviness in her heart as I recounted my fears. I knew that she was the one person who understood.

We cried, and held each other, and when the moment felt right, I said goodbye. I felt the door of the conversation—the door that had still felt open the last time I left her house—close behind me as a sign of completion.

As I drove home after that second meeting, I realized the Universe had found a way to heal the wounds of the past. The silent agony my mother had harbored in her heart for most of her life had been liberated. There in her kitchen, my mother had finally had the opportunity to voice the pain and suffering she had been forced to bear in silence.

I also found context for so much of what I had struggled with myself—both in recent months and throughout my life. I understood my fear of the dark and my terror at the thought of sexual assault. I understood why I felt paralyzed by my fear, unable to move, just as my mother had felt overpowered by her attacker. And I understood why my throat chakra was closed, why I struggled so much to express myself. It was the very same silence that had been forced upon my mother.

Over the next several days, my emotional processing was replaced with a series of questions. My mother had provided a good deal of information, but it wasn't particularly detailed—likely both because it was painful to remember and the many years that have lapsed.

My questions varied. How long had she known the man who assaulted her? When, and how, did my grandmother find out? What had happened to the baby? Was she still in Trinidad? Did anyone else in the family know her? My brother, sister, and I had a half-sibling, but where was she? Who else knew about this happening? When did they find out, and how? Who took the baby in? Who took my mother in? How many people were wrapped up in this story, and could I find any of them today?

But by far the most burning question was about what had become of the man who raped my mother. I was still desperate for confirmation that he shared a soul with Diana. If he died before Diana was born, at least I could confirm that it was possible. This seemed like the most important thing to rule out.

I couldn't ask my mother these things. It no longer felt right, or compassionate. So I called my brother and asked him instead. Did he know anything else about the story, or the identity of Granny's partner? My brother was forthright with what he knew but admitted that, in the scope of things, it was quite limited. He suggested I speak with other family members. My next move was to begin calling my mother's siblings. I just wanted the man's name; if I had it, I could look for public records of his death. But everyone else in my family was tight-lipped. They didn't want to share anything with me—in fact, it seemed like they actively wanted to keep me from pursuing the information.

At this point, different parts of me wanted different things. There was the part that wanted to know everything and wouldn't stop until I had all the information. This part of me couldn't rest until I knew all facets of the truth. Why did my family hold so many secrets? I thought back to all the unknowns in my family's past. I know nothing about my family in the generations before my grandmother; no one does, because no one ever talked about it.

There was another part of me that wanted to trust the download itself. *What more proof do I need?* this version of me wondered. I had already received the sign I had asked for in discovering Diana's birthday *on* her birthday, and I had received confirmation when I drew the card bearing her name from Kyle's deck. Why couldn't I just trust in that? Perhaps, I thought, I would never ever be satisfied; perhaps the issue was not that I lacked information, but rather that I lacked trust. I thought back to Diana's unconditional acceptance of what I had shared with her days before. What would it take to just believe?

A third part of me was protective and wanted to shelter my mother, as well as the rest of the family, from this painful information. I had seen the discomfort and fear in my mother's demeanor that day at the kitchen table. Though she gave the information freely, it troubled her to do so. I asked myself why I still needed to know. What would I accomplish by getting more details? Whom would it serve? Certainly not my mother, who was the one most hurt by the events of the past; why not protect her from further pain in the here and now?

With all three parts of me speaking at once, it was hard to move forward with my questions. I made a few fruitless phone calls, but I contemplated them on my own much more. The process was lonely. I couldn't reach out to Diana; for the first time, I really didn't want to do so. But the idea that I had caused her pain still bothered me; what if my sharing had hurt her? On the human level, it seems logical that the victims are more hurt by misdeeds than the perpetrators. On the soul level, though, I think this is overly simplistic. It causes us great harm to do harm to others. It hurts the soul and leaves a wound to heal. Were there still things to untangle between me and Diana? Worse, had my sharing *created* more entanglement or blocks? Without seeing her, there was no way to know.

The week that followed was confusing. I had still told no one in my personal life about the events that had occurred. The only people who knew what I had been through were Diana and, to some extent, John Newton. In my isolation, I began to feel anxious. The relief of knowing what had happened to my mother in her own words and delivering my grandmother's message to her was tempered by my concern for Diana.

Late one night, unable to sleep, I began to compose an email.

Dear Diana,

I am so grateful for the journey we took together. I absolutely believe in divine orchestration because without it, I would not have met you.

At the same time, I'm a little bit worried about how our conversation may have affected you. I still want to make sure there are no negative charges or hurts between us, in this lifetime or in any other. Could we have one more session together, but instead of you giving me a healing, we offer healing to each other? You do hands-on healing, but for me it comes through prayer. I would like to offer a prayer for us, with your permission. Are you open to receiving it?

Many blessings,

Judi

I hit send and waited a few minutes. Then, her response landed in my inbox. I was grateful that she'd responded so quickly. We set a time and a date for several weeks out—enough time that we could both process what had transpired. Then, knowing that we would meet again to heal any potential charges remaining between us, I fell straight into the deepest sleep I'd had in a long time. I had closed the cycle with my mother by delivering my grandmother's message. Now, it was time to close the cycle with Diana.

Chapter Eleven

Forever Changed

I sat in my office, blankly staring at my never-ending list of things to do and half-listening to the conversation taking place in the adjacent hall. I wasn't thinking about anything in particular when I felt the unmistakable pang of emotion tug at my heart. I closed my eyes, took a deep inhale in, holding it for a few beats before slowly and deliberately releasing it. Then the tears began to well up. Remaining calm and composed, I quickly rose out of my chair and walked over to the door, quietly shutting it against the busy scene in the hallway. It was fine, I told myself; no one would judge me, they would just think I was in a particularly strong moment of focus. But in truth, I needed privacy. I needed the safety of knowing I wouldn't be seen or judged.

Only when the door was closed did I let my tears fall.

As I cried, I went through a familiar set of steps. One by one, I felt the sensations move through my body and release. As they did, I let them go without giving any of them a name—without sticking them inside a story of my own creation. Outside, the leaves were exploding with the color and life of spring. They would flourish through the summer only to dry and fall again in the autumn—like me—releasing everything.

Sometimes, this is easy. Other times, it is more of a challenge. When I struggle, I hold on to the tools I know well—the prayers, meditations, and other techniques I have gathered over the course of the last year, many of which I offer in this narrative.

In the days that followed my revelation, I was as raw and open as I had ever been. I had spent most of my life building up walls around my heart to protect me from anything that might have caused me harm. In the course of a few short months, those walls had come crashing down—or, better yet, I had torn them down with my own hands. I had no regrets about this. Their destruction was intentional; I knew that the walls that had once protected me were now only holding me back. But without them, I felt completely unprotected from the outside; completely exposed.

I was relatively private about this process. I was living in a state of emotional overwhelm. I was at full capacity, and at the slightest provocation, my emotions would start to spill out beyond my control. Usually, this happened in the form of tears, but sometimes it was just sensations.

My heart felt wide open, there for the world to see. I was acutely aware that having my heart open was a feeling I had once known. It came back to me like a memory, something I had long forgotten. And I also knew I had missed it; I felt a fondness for it, becoming aware of how much I had longed for its return.

It was as if I had been sitting in the dark, occasionally allowing a crack of light to come in through the window shade, until suddenly the curtain was pulled back and the room was filled with light. In those months, I was just there, blinking, shocked by its brilliance. I was walking around, living my regular life the same as always. But on the inside, I was just trying to show up for the emotional process that was unfolding.

Something I could not name had undeniably shifted within me. I had spent much of my life subconsciously turning away from my emotions, just as I had turned away from the downloads and visitations I experienced as a child. It was just fear; it was only ever fear. Again and again, I sat with my fear, daring to stay present despite it. Daring to turn toward it and keep breathing.

I cried many tears in the days following my revelation and the subsequent conversations with both my mother and Diana. As I experience them, tears of joy and tears of sadness are the same thing. Or, at least, they are for me. They feel the same in my body, they both spring from my eyes in precisely the same way. It's the story we give to the experience that causes us to label them as "happiness," "sadness," or anything else. There's nothing inherently good or inherently bad about tears, or even emotions themselves; good and bad are only governed by the stories we give them. Knowing this, I allowed myself to feel the immense power of my own heart and let each separate sensation flow through me. And as they did, I slowly began to feel lighter. The sensations, feelings, and tears cleansed me. An awareness descended. Or, perhaps, I ascended into an awareness that had long been waiting for me. Somehow, in some realm my mind has no ability to understand, I knew I was releasing the burdens of the past.

In these moments of awareness, I felt as though I understood everything—the perfection of the Universe was so clear, and I was filled with gratitude for being able to see it. Once these moments of clarity passed, doubt would seem to descend on me again. I couldn't shake the idea that having real-world proof of the plausibility of my revelation would help put my insecurities to rest. Sometimes, I would take this urge as far as making phone calls to my family members, trying to surreptitiously dig up information from a cousin or an aunt. I didn't want to hurt my mother by dredging up the past, *but,* I thought, *surely someone knows something that could help reassure me that Diana at least could be a reincarnation of Granny's former partner.* So gingerly, I would pick up the phone and ask some vague questions about my family's past in Trinidad.

These attempts weren't very fruitful. I didn't know who knew what, so I constantly had to dance around the questions I actually wanted to ask to avoid accidentally revealing something new. Meanwhile, those who *did* know seemed determined to keep their secrets. The process was frustrating and confusing. And I kept hearing the two other parts of me—the one that wanted me to trust in the guidance I had received, and the one that wanted to protect my mother—all along the way. I would remember the unbelievable synchronicity of Diana's birthday, followed by the direct message the oracle card bearing her name sent, and wonder why I needed this sort of confirmation. Had not the Universe already provided me with enough?

As time progressed, I began to spend more time firm in my faith and less time shaking in doubt. In the end, I decided that though there is a part of me that still does want to know if my revelation is true, I will let that piece lie dormant. The damage and hurt I could inflict by continuing to ask was just too much. It's natural to want to know all the details, but they actually serve the mind much more than the heart, and I've made the choice to live from my heart. I never found out the man's name, let alone the date of his death, and as of this writing, I still know nothing about the identity or whereabouts of my half-sister. If these details unfold on their own, I welcome them. If they don't, it's okay, too. I no longer need to know all of what happened. And I don't need confirmation of the connection between Diana and the man who hurt my mother, because in my heart I already know.

I also know that for me, secrets are no longer the way forward. I understand why people keep them. I certainly understand why my mother kept hers. I feel how a secret contracts my heart. Secrets hold a weight that I just no longer have the strength, or will, to carry. They push me into the past, and I am determined to remain in the present.

Every family struggles with some darkness. In the case of my family, secrets were a part of our shadow. We're not alone in that. So maybe this is how we heal: By bringing things to the surface and releasing them, just as we do with our own emotions. Maybe this is how, as some Native American cultures believe, we facilitate the healing our family needs, seven generations back and seven generations forward. We give voice to everyone who went unheard—in this case, the fear, shock, and grief of a twelve-year-old girl. And no matter how much it may hurt us to hear the pain in that voice, to hear the heartbreak and the trauma that has been borne in silence, we keep our hearts open as best we can.

We do this because when we open our hearts, we inspire others to do the same. We show them what is possible and, consciously or subconsciously, they open their hearts a little more too. Seven generations forward. Seven generations back. And also in this lifetime, rippling outward to everyone we meet.

Shortly after my pivotal conversations with both Diana and my mother, I had the opportunity to meet with John Newton again. I didn't hesitate. As soon as I saw the event invitation in my inbox, I signed up for a private session.

There was no way to explain everything that had happened. For one thing, the session wasn't nearly long enough for that, and for another, I still didn't have the words to describe it. That inquiry would take me quite some time—apparently, it would take me an entire book. But I did want to thank him. I wanted him to know that his work had touched me deeply and that he had played a pivotal role in my family's healing. John says he isn't a healer; he's emphatic about it, and I respect that. John is forever humble. He says he gets out of the way to allow the Creator to come through. To me, it is a clearing of the pains, burdens, and stories that we've been carrying around. I believe he's an incredibly gifted facilitator and I felt called to tell him that.

As our session began, I thanked John and told him that our previous session had profoundly impacted me. Not only that, I explained, it helped free a group of souls from the burdens they had been carrying for decades.

I told him, again, what had happened to my mother, and I offered a little background on my work with Diana, my hysterectomy, my struggle to express myself, and the call I had received on Good Friday. John listened patiently as I connected all the dots.

Then I reminded him of what he had told me in our first session: That everything would unfold in perfect timing, and that it was right in front of me. I explained my revelation about Diana's connection to my family. And I described the sensations I experienced as the emotions moved through me. Then, John jumped in to confirm what I already knew: That the key to all of this was that I didn't try to make a story about these events. Instead, I just experienced them and let them go. By doing that, he said, *everything* could flow. The story and the burdens of the past were cleansed and washed out to sea, leaving us all free.

"It's like a tsunami," John explained. "A boat can be hundreds of miles offshore, and as long as there's nothing out there for it to hit, it isn't destroyed by even the largest wave; it just rises up with the water and settles back down again. The wave passes, and the boat remains."

As the conversation ended, John did his forgiveness prayer. As he finished, I joined him with "Please and thank you."

It had been several weeks since I had last seen Diana. As I drove up to her house, I observed her neighborhood in full bloom. Spring was turning to summer.

Spencer was calm when I got there. After greeting me, he lay still on his bed.

Diana herself felt open to my presence that day, though something had changed between us.

"I'm happy to see you," she affirmed out of the silence, smiling warmly to dismiss my concerns.

"And I am glad to hear it." My answer was honest; I had been worried about what she might think of me, whether she still believed me, and whether she was hurt by what I had shared. I pulled the picture book I had brought out of my bag. "Do you remember *The Little Soul and the Sun?*"

She nodded as I held the cover up for her to see. From the back of the book, Neale Donald Walsch's face smiled at me.

As it turned out, the book I had given Diana after our second session together, the very book I held in my hand, foretold our entire journey. I asked her if I could read parts of it to her, and she agreed. As I began to flip through the pages and read the story aloud, I could see in her eyes that she was beginning to understand the connection I was trying to make.

The book tells of a conversation between God and a little soul that is between lifetimes. God asks the little soul what he wants to experience and he answers, "Forgiveness." Since there is only perfection and nothing to forgive, God asks him how he will experience it, and a beautiful angel of light comes forth to volunteer her help. The little soul asks why she would do such a thing and she explains that she will do it because she loves him. As I moved through the book with Diana, she became increasingly emotional, and when I got to the part about the angel performing this task out of love, I saw the first tears spring to her eyes.

I went on, my voice choked and beginning to waver, and I read the part where the angel of light asks the little soul to remind her of this on Earth. She would need a reminder, the angel explained, because she would be pretending so hard to be what she is not that she was likely to forget. At this, Diana's eyes filled completely.

I continued to read. There, in the heavens, the agreement is made. Then, God sends both the little soul and the angel of light to Earth to live out their lessons.

By the time I finished the story, Diana was so emotional that she could hardly speak. After some time, she was able to form a simple sentence: "You know who I am."

The air around us both was heavy with emotion born out of a profound and exquisite love. Everything had come together perfectly.

Because it is perfect. We're *all* perfect, as Neale's book shows; we're beings of light here to learn. And that requires context, because we can't experience our perfection until we know the opposite. We can't know light without darkness, good without bad. Diana's soul and mine had come into this world together in order to learn something, and by doing so in the highest possible way, without creating blocks, we had learned it.

I closed the back cover of the book, holding it firmly in my lap, and took a deep breath. "You see?" I asked. "I always knew we were connected and now, I understand how. Of course, we can't be sure—we can never be sure. But *what if?*"

After a few more quiet breaths together, we both stood up and moved toward the healing table.

Diana gave me the final hands-on healing that day. Her hands felt warm and, unlike the last time, I didn't need a blanket. Everything that had felt incomplete before came full circle on the healing table, as she moved from my feet to my crown. I had an overwhelming sense of wholeness and finality.

Spencer slept through the entire proceeding. I had come to see him as a kindred spirit. He was always deeply connected to the energy between me and Diana, or perhaps all the energy in the room. We weren't in there alone; we were always accompanied by something greater.

I settled into the yellow recliner. Spine straight, Diana was composed in her office chair as ever, though her eyes were heavy with emotion. "You said you wanted to offer me a prayer?" she said, her pitch rising on the final word to make it a question.

"Yes. I want to do John Newton's forgiveness prayer together."

I think she was surprised by that. "Why? Why do you want to do this prayer?"

I didn't quite know how to answer. "I just think it will be good to clear any charge that might still be lingering," I said slowly.

"Is there a charge for you?" she asked. We had both used the word "charge," but I knew what we meant: *Was I upset by my revelation? Did I hold a grudge against her, or did I feel betrayal, anger or fear?* Both of us had the same concern about the other: Could we continue to send each other love, despite all that had happened, or was it just too muddled now?

I took a breath before answering. I wanted to be in my absolute highest truth. Eyes closed, I felt into my whole body, my whole being. I released a long, slow exhale and opened my eyes.

"For me, no."

She looked at me quizzically, as if it was an answer she didn't expect. Then she said something surprising: "Nothing upsets you."

Her pitch didn't rise this time; it wasn't a question. It wasn't a judgment, either. Instead, it was a simple observation: *Nothing upsets you.* There was something else in it, though, which is hard for me to describe even today.

If I had to pick a single word, I would say it was *awe*.

As always, she believed me. She knew I was telling the truth and that there was no charge. I was showing up open, understanding, loving, and compassionate; I was bringing my highest self. I was experiencing the emotion of it without creating a story, and because of that, any charge that might have formed was rendered obsolete.

"I know you were afraid to share this with me," she said. Again, it wasn't a question. She was right; sharing had not been easy. "Why was that?" she went on. "Was it because you thought that by sharing it, you would hurt me?"

This time, I didn't hesitate: "Yes," I answered. "And I'm sorry."

Diana's eyes burned like fire, her piercing gaze landing right in my heart. "There's nothing to be sorry for," she said. After a moment, she repeated it again, more slowly this time. "There's nothing to be sorry for, Judi. *Nothing at all.*"

I took a minute to let it really sink in before responding.

"I'm so glad to hear it," I finally answered. "And I need you to know that though we're going to do this forgiveness prayer together, I don't have anything to forgive. I understand forgiveness in a whole new way now. As I understand it, we are never condemned in the Creator's eyes because we are unconditionally loved. I don't need to forgive you, because I never created a story or blamed you. I just let the sensations move through me without labels or judgements. So please understand, this prayer isn't even about you and me. It will clear any blocks that anyone has around this, anywhere, in either of our lineages."

She seemed relieved, and I could relate; each of us had harbored some level of concern that the other might be hurt by the revelation. I watched as she accepted my words into her heart.

She was the one who had come to teach me about forgiveness. She was the angel of light, from Neale Donald Walsch's book, who had pretended so hard to be what she was not that she needed this lifetime to heal it.

With that, I knew it was time for the forgiveness prayer.

First, I closed my eyes and said John's prayer in silence from memory. Then, I recited it aloud.

> *Infinite Creator, all that you are ...*
> *Please and thank you. Please and thank you. Please and thank you.*

I asked her if there was anything else for us to clear before I left, and she said no. I felt the same; there was a strong sense of finality surrounding us.

As Diana walked me to the door and watched me say goodbye to Spencer, I knew we were complete. We had fulfilled our agreement with each other; we had cleared the blocks from our family lines. For months, I had felt inexplicably drawn to Diana. Long after I was healed from the trauma my body underwent during the hysterectomy, I continued to come for some sort of other healing that my heart demanded but I couldn't quite articulate, even to myself. I now understood I had been carrying a burden I simply could not release on my own: One which predated this incarnation. That burden, too, had been set free. I no longer felt pulled back to Diana's office or her table. I knew I wouldn't return.

As the freedom that accompanied that truth set in, I felt only love.

I walked to my car, marveling at the perfection of the Universe and all the beauty it contains.

Light is the highest vibration in the Universe, and because we are all made of light, we are united within it—a human tribe spanning the generations, separate beings with separate lifetimes who share this common essence. And within that essence, we are united, we are one.

In our densest, human form, this light manifests as love. We are here to remember who and what we are. This is a process, because part of our divine agreement is that sometimes, we will pretend to be what we are not. Sometimes, we will move out of alignment, making choices with our free will that don't match up with who we truly are, which is love. It's then up to us to take responsibility for our misstep, to heal, and to release the negative stories of our past.

Diana and I made a divine agreement, and together, we fulfilled it. I drove home that day thinking of her statement, "You know who I am," over and over. I've thought about that sentence a lot in the time that has passed. And I've realized that there are, in fact, several ways to interpret it. Perhaps she wanted to remind me of this incarnation as Diana, the healer living in suburban America. Perhaps she wanted to remind me of her past incarnation as an unnamed man living in Trinidad in the 1950s. Perhaps both. But I still choose to interpret it as I initially did, that day in her office: I choose to believe that she was referring to the "I" that my soul recognized from between lives, when we settled on a set of lessons to go through together.

I will go on learning, surrounded by souls who are here to teach me. I will know many of them from before, though it's likely that I'll forget most. I'll only know what we came here to learn together once we've learned it, because that's how we agreed it would be before we arrived.

And as I go through this set of lessons, I won't be alone. As the whispered voice told me, "If you knew who stood beside you, you would never be afraid." For me, it is the Creator who walks with me, and my angels and guides are there, ready to assist. Once I ask for help, I can release and surrender to the outcome—because I know that I am not alone. I can understand that stories rarely serve; true emotional processing is a set of sensations, and when I don't try to label them, they flow through me more easily.

In the months that followed that final meeting, I began to feel that Diana and I needed to create something together in order to share this experience with the world. Maybe seeing what we went through together could help others, showing them one way to approach their own challenges with the broader perspective of many lifetimes: the lifetimes in which we misstep and the lifetimes in which we heal. As the seeds of this book began to emerge, I wondered if we might co-write it, telling our story together. But as I began to record everything that happened, it became clear that we *had* already written the story together, just like the divine agreement between the little soul and the angel of light. By living it, Diana and I had created a living, breathing thing, and now it was up to me to write it all down.

Midway through writing this book, I sat down to compose one of my last emails to Diana:

Dear Diana,

My human mind struggles to understand all of this, but my heart tells me that everything has been divinely orchestrated.

I first came to you for my physical ailments, but I have been healed on so many levels. I have learned to feel more; to find my voice; to be freed from the fears of the past; and to know and experience the love of the Universe.

I have been healed, and for this I give my eternal thanks. Thank you.

I love you,

Judi

Her response was timely and kind. Though we exchanged a few more emails after that, we never regained the relationship we had once had. Our work together is finished.

Part Three Integration

Reflections

We are so much more than our physical bodies. We are energetic beings made of light. And each of us is also a part of a deeply interconnected grouping of souls, linked through our DNA. In one respect, we are the sum of our ancestors; we carry their triumphs and traumas in our very cells. Yet we are more than that, too. We are also spiritual beings with free will, and our actions reverberate forward and backward through the generations.

Most of this happens unconsciously. We are beings of love who were born with our hearts wide open, but we naturally close them to protect ourselves from a world that scares us. We may create negative stories about the events around us to understand them, but unfortunately, these stories can close our hearts and keep us from truly feeling. We stop feeling our emotions as bodily sensations, relying on our stories as substitutes instead. Our negative stories often give meaning to the events of our lives, which in turn may cause blocks that prevent the love and light of the Creator from totally reaching us. We cling so tightly to our stories that they often become our identity—and then, we become too afraid to let them go.

Our spiritual growth begins when we choose to drop our stories and start opening our hearts again, remembering who we truly are.

As we do so, the fears and burdens that block us begin to drop away. We begin to feel our emotions as sensations and process things more quickly.

This process is not always easy. And it can sometimes feel quite lonely. It's easy to get fooled by the events of our daily lives and label them. But when we do that, we limit their potential to set us free.

It is on this journey that I came to experience and understand how forgiveness works. Now I know that in the eyes of the Creator we are never condemned. Forgiveness is never necessary because we are unconditionally loved and accepted for who we are, exactly as we are. Forgiveness is a gift we give ourselves. It allows us to release the contracted energies that are holding us back and allows us to move forward. We forgive the negative stories we have created around the events of our lives. We transform those stories of judgement, blame, fear, and doubt into love.

This doesn't mean we condone the actions that have hurt us. Instead, we see them as part of a greater process. We see them as opportunities to look at the world through the Creator's eyes, to see each other as angels of light, and to see each misstep as part of the path toward greater healing.

Though we are divine beings, we are also having human experiences. And that means we have free will to choose—including choices that take us out of our alignment. That means truly traumatic events may occur, leaving overwhelming pain in their wake. But it can serve us to understand that these events can be part of our divine agreement or a greater plan. What if everything that happens is actually here to serve us? Choosing to look at it this way can give our pain a spiritual context that brings us relief.

We can begin to touch one of the highest spiritual truths, which is also often one of the hardest to see: That everything is perfect. Everything is part of the divine agreement we made before we came here. Everything is here to serve us.

So, in the same way I did at the very beginning of this narrative, I invite you to simply ask yourself: "What if? What if that were true?"

"What if?" allows us to be open to an alternative possibility and to release the stories that no longer serve us. I released several of my own over the course of this narrative. First, by opening to my spiritual gifts and refusing to shut down the part of me that sees spirits and receives guidance from beyond, I came to embrace the ways in which I am different. Once I embraced this part of me, I no longer needed to fight my differences or feel victimized by them, as I learned through Miriam's message after she passed away.

As I slowly unraveled each of these stories, I was given the biggest test of all in the revelation itself. I had the opportunity to create a story. Instead, led by higher guidance, I chose to use the revelation as an opportunity to bring healing and light to the whole family line. Through our interactions together, Diana and I were both freed.

It's fitting that this inquiry began on Good Friday. It's also fitting that it, in many ways, ended on a birthday—Diana's. Both show us that we can be reborn into a new reality the second we choose to look at things differently. Part of my ego died and was born as something higher. This is available to all of us; we only need to get into our bodies and into our hearts, and let our stories dissolve.

This makes space for healing, not only if we are the ones who are hurt but also if we are the ones who use our free will to misstep. When that happens, our soul is given the opportunity to heal it, either in this lifetime or the next. I believe that this is what happened for Diana. By reincarnating as my healer, she took responsibility for her misstep and made peace with her soul's difficult past.

I received so many lessons through this experience that I really struggled to funnel them all into this one book. Luckily, I'm still learning. I will likely go through this process many more times, as will you. We will both have more chances to remember how forgiveness works. We will both create stories again, despite our best intentions, and we will both be blessed with the opportunity to let them go. We do this by transforming them through love and finding the perfection in the situation.

All of the above is part of a greater process. It's a precise recipe that brought us here; it's the agreement that our souls made with each other.

I face the future knowing what my highest self is capable of, and what is possible when we really believe that we always have an opportunity to heal. Every misstep holds the promise of an opportunity to make it right. Every burden we carry holds the potential to be released.

This is what I mean when I say that we really, truly can't get it wrong.

Exercises

What If?

We are often so caught up in our stories that we can't see things from a broader perspective. We become identified with these stories, causing unnecessary pain. Questions are a great way of stepping back and taking a greater view of life's events.

Sometimes, I found this easy and almost automatic. Other times, it took more work. I began to work with a set of questions when I was tempted to create a story and react to it:

1. What if the event that caused so much hurt is actually here to serve me?

2. What positive lesson could I have learned from it if I was willing to let go of my anger, pain, or frustration?

3. If I could see it from the other person's perspective, what might that look like?

4. What can I find to appreciate about the event, the other person, or myself?

5. What if the perpetrator of this wrongdoing were someone I loved? What compassion and understanding could I show them?

6. In moments of great tragedy or conflict, our minds often struggle to make sense of it all. However, when we are able to put aside our pain and open our hearts with compassion and love, we are often able to collectively come together as one. In that state, a greater consciousness happens and positive change can occur. What is that positive change?

7. When would I be willing to let go and forgive? Before I die? In ten years? In five years?

8. Why am I waiting? What do I need to do, say, or release in order to do it now?

These questions were of great service to me, and they may be to you, as well, whether you address them in your journal, out loud to a coach or a friend, or just ponder them as you go about your day—maybe, like me, on your long commute. Anytime we can take a minute to connect with ourselves, it brings us closer to rediscovering the truth of who we are.

Calling in the Creator

We live in a loving and supportive Universe. We are never alone, never abandoned, always loved. We can access the Creator and this divine love at any moment through our hearts. It is through the many forms of love (such as gratitude, forgiveness, compassion) that we can access the power of our hearts. Tapping into these higher vibrations or frequencies allows our lives to expand more quickly. Journaling is a great way to consciously bring this awareness to the forefront of our lives, because what we appreciate increases.

Journal on these three topics and note how your life begins to make more and more positive shifts.

1. Love. Love is the essence of who you are. You need to reconnect to your true eternal self by letting go of the stories and experiencing life through the eyes of love. Let love and your heart be the compass that guides you forward. Who or what can you love in your life? Where can you let love lead?

2. Gratitude. Go through all the moments of your life thankful for what you've been blessed with. The Universe will rush in to provide you with even more because what you focus on expands. What can you be grateful for?

3. Forgiveness. Forgiveness is a gift you give yourself. It allows you to let go of all the contracted energy and stories that you hold in your body. It allows you to let go of the past so you can embrace the now. What can you start letting go of?

We can access the Creator through our hearts but also through the power of prayer. Both of the following prayers have been very important to me throughout this process. Neither of them require a specific religious background, or any religious background at all; they are compatible with all spiritual belief systems. You can pray quietly in the morning when you wake up or at night. You can also pray throughout the day, whenever the need arises.

Ho'oponopono

The Ho'oponopono prayer is a Hawaiian forgiveness ritual that is designed to bring peace and harmony to both the person that is praying as well as to those around them.

The true power of this prayer was demonstrated by Ihaleakala Hew Len, PhD. In the book, *Zero Limits,* that he co-wrote with Dr. Joe Vitale, Dr. Len describes his experience working in a facility for the criminally insane. It was a violent ward and many of the patients had to be restrained. Rather than meet the patients face-to-face, Dr. Len reviewed each case file in his office and then practiced the Ho'oponopono prayer. His belief was that in taking 100 percent responsibility for himself he would be able to heal himself, and in doing so, heal others. As the months went by, the patients became calmer and their restraints were removed. Within three years of Dr. Len's continued practice with the Ho'oponopono prayer, the ward was closed since it was no longer needed.

Is there a situation in your life that could benefit from the Ho'oponopono prayer? It can be used to release any resentment or anger toward a person or a situation or it can even be directed toward yourself. Try this:

1. Find a quiet space and get comfortable.

2. Close your eyes and call to mind the person or the situation that is causing you discomfort.

3. Spend a few minutes calmly reciting the Ho'oponopono prayer, picturing that person in front of you. Simply recite:

   I am sorry.

   Please forgive me.

   Thank you.

   I love you.

4. If you are working on forgiving yourself, call up an image of yourself sitting in front of you.

5. Repeat the process daily for a few weeks.

6. Notice a sense of lightness and spaciousness that you start to feel when thinking about yourself or that person.

John Newton's Forgiveness Prayer

I included this prayer in the narrative, but I am reprinting it here because it has brought me so much solace. As with the Ho'oponopono and the Lord's Prayer, I often find myself reciting the words of John Newton's forgiveness prayer throughout my day. There is a power that comes with mentally repeating a prayer over and over. It rewires our unconscious to align with the prayer. And note that just like the Ho'oponopono, it includes love, forgiveness, gratitude, and calling in the Creator.

Reading or speaking John's forgiveness prayer connects you to the Creator, the true source of all health and well-being. It is encoded with a direct connection to consciousness itself and the intelligence structured within it.

> *Infinite Creator, All That You Are: For me, all my family members, all our relationships, all our ancestors and all their relationships through all time, through all our lives ...*
>
> *For all hurts and wrongs: Physical, mental, emotional, spiritual, sexual and financial through thought, word or deed: Please help*

us all forgive each other, forgive ourselves, forgive all people and all people forgive us, completely and totally. Please and thank you.

For all suicide, incest, murder, rape, abortion and infidelity through thought, word or deed: Please help us all forgive each other, forgive ourselves, forgive all people and all people forgive us, completely and totally. Please and thank you.

For all times we abandoned or were abandoned; withheld love or had love withheld; weren't nurtured, loved and supported and times we didn't nurture love or support others: Infinite Creator, please help us all forgive, be forgiven and all forgive ourselves, completely and totally. Please and thank you.

Please, Infinite Creator, for the highest good: Lift out all weight, pain, burden, sin, death, debt, negativity and limitation of all kinds; transform it into your love, and let your love flow back into us, filling and giving us all complete peace, now and forever. Please and thank you. Please and thank you. Please and thank you.

Please help us love and bless each other; love and bless ourselves. Be at peace with each other and at peace with ourselves, now and forever. Please and thank you.

John, forever humble, offers a special thanks to visionary Howard Wills for his inspiration and pioneering forgiveness work.

May these words be of service to you, as they have so often helped me—even in ways I still can't fully understand. Like all the best truths in life, this prayer continues to unfold for me. I wish the same for you.

Epilogue

As I turn onto the highway, I notice that the first autumn leaves are starting to fall. In the background, a song I haven't heard before is playing, part of an automatically generated playlist of tracks some software thinks I might like. Around me, other commuters survey their options and switch on their turn signals, merging into the lanes around them. For a moment, I see us all driving together as one force, a pure stream of cars and their passengers headed toward a common goal. Yet each one of us is individual, separate; in the end, each one of us goes our own way.

Straight ahead, I see a sign marking the exit for Diana's house. One mile, the sign warns; half a mile, says the next. As I pass the turnoff, the song ends. There's a pause, and then a single chord plays through the stereo. Ed Sheeran's voice breaks through, singing "Perfect."

My car sails past the edge of Diana's neighborhood. I still feel a small sensation in my chest when it does; not one that signifies baggage from the past, but one that indicates how much we experienced together. Sometimes this sensation even brings me to tears as I contemplate the profound meaning of it all, but not today. Today, the sensation is gentle. I breathe into it and exhale gratitude, sending love to Diana, Spencer, and all the angels and guides who accompanied us along the way.

As Ed's voice washes over me, I overflow with emotion—not good, not bad, just emotion. I let the sensation move through me and then, just like that, it passes. Gone.

It has been two years since I first met Diana. It has been one year since I saw her last, at our final meeting when we did John Newton's forgiveness prayer together. This last year has been instrumental for me. I have made major life changes, dedicating much of my time and energy to creating this account of what she and I experienced together. I know that the final stage of this story is for me to share it with the world.

In the last two years, I've had the opportunity to unravel so many of the stories I created. In their absence, I've been able to envision something new. I stared down my own story about being different. In it, I found some truth. I am different from other people in some ways, but I'm not in others. Moreover, the ways in which I am different can be celebrated. I have unique gifts to bring to the world, just like everyone else, and I am no longer willing to hold them back in order to fit in. I am no longer afraid of being different. Instead, I embrace it. I welcome it as part of what makes me who I am.

I struggled significantly with a feeling that something was missing—that I was incomplete somehow. I now see that the thing that was missing was my heart; that rediscovering how to live *from* the heart was an integral part of my journey. Because on the other end of that, I remembered who I am.

I saw how everything could come full circle and be perfect, and I was able to see myself in the same way. I am just as I should be; I am complete and whole. Without a story to tell me otherwise, nothing is missing at all.

The version of me who first walked into Diana's office had so much trouble expressing herself. At the time, I didn't know how to use my voice. And while expression still doesn't always come easily to me, I don't resist it anymore. My throat chakra is unblocked—I can speak,

I can sing, and I can be heard, too. Sure, sometimes I still get stuck, but overall, the latent anxiety that accompanied my story about self-expression has dissolved, and I am left with my clear, vibrant voice—even if it's still a little off-key sometimes. That's just one more thing for me to embrace. It's the small imperfection that is part of the greater perfection.

Releasing these stories helped me to let go of even wider, more overarching stories I was holding about being unsafe and being alone. The stronger I become emotionally, the less afraid I am.

Furthermore, I'm not afraid of my fear anymore; wherever I still have fear, I also have confidence that I will be the one to face it. I know that I'm guided at every step; the Creator and the Universe itself are watching over me.

I know that I am not alone, never abandoned, always loved.

My experiences with Diana, which acted in parallel with the process of opening my heart, demonstrated for me what is truly possible when we refuse to create a story in the first place. The tools I used along the way were invaluable in this process. It is my sincere hope that you can use them, too, as you face your own challenges.

As it turns out, we can face even the greatest challenge if we just process the emotions as they arise, feeling them as sensations without labels. And this understanding holds within it the greatest lesson of all: That forgiveness is truly a gift we give to ourselves. Forgiveness washes away the stories, the pain, and the darkness, leaving only love behind. It reunites us with the Creator, who never has to forgive, because we are never condemned. Whenever we misstep, moving out of alignment with our true self, we have the opportunity to heal in this lifetime or in any other. We need only choose to do so.

As this narrative began, I wrote that the entire Universe is a complicated, interconnected web of events and energies, all of it perfectly designed. It's like a jigsaw puzzle, I explained; there may be uneven edges, missing pieces or even holes in the picture here and there, but as those final pieces snap into place, the perfection of the whole becomes obvious.

What if, like a jigsaw puzzle, there are no wrong pieces? What if each one has its place in the whole?

When we look at life that way, everything changes. Everything shifts. Suddenly, we see the world as it really is: Perfect.

Additional Resources

My mentors and teachers have blessed my life with their wisdom and guidance. I've listed their websites below as you may find them helpful on your own journey.

Janet Bray Attwood, www.thepassiontest.com

Sonia Choquette, www.soniachoquette.com

Dr. Wayne Dyer, www.drwaynedyer.com

Lisa Garr, www.theawareshow.com

Kasey Mathews, www.kaseymathews.com

Dr. Sue Morter, www.drsuemorter.com

John Newton, www.healthbeyondbelief.com

Debra Poneman, www.yestosuccess.com

Marci Shimoff, www.happyfornoreason.com and www.youryearofmiracles.com

Acknowledgements

I give my eternal thanks to my family, past and present, for their unconditional love and support. I am blessed that you accompany me every step of the way.

Thank you to all my angels and guides, in the seen and the unseen. I know that I am never alone and always loved.

Thank you to my mentors, teachers, Year of Miracles family, and Happy for No Reason sisters for their wisdom, guidance, and encouragement. I extend a special thanks to Marci Shimoff, Debra Poneman, John Newton, Sonia Choquette, Dr. Sue Morter, Janet Bray Attwood, Dr. Wayne Dyer, Lisa Garr, Suzanne Lawlor, Leila Reyes, Kasey Mathews, Kim Forcina, and Shauna Hardy.

To Diana, for always believing and accepting me exactly as I am. Thank you for taking this incredible healing journey with me and for helping me experience the perfection of all that is.

To Chandika Devi for your amazing words that always inspire me. Thank you for helping me get this message out into the world.

Thank you to Geoff Affleck and Nina Shoroplova for all of their help and support.

I am eternally grateful to all of you. All my love.

About Judi Miller

Born in Trinidad, Judi immigrated to the United States as a child. She started her career as a Certified Public Accountant and went on to excel in the world of corporate finance while raising two children with her loving husband.

Most of her life has been dedicated to personal development and helping others excel in a constantly changing environment. Over the past several years, Judi's interest shifted toward spirituality. Her growth was no longer aimed at making herself better; instead, she began to focus on finding her intrinsic wholeness. This shift brought her numerous lessons around the nature of the Creator, forgiveness, and the trajectory each soul follows throughout the course of many lives.

Today, sharing these lessons is an integral part of her journey. As a coach, speaker, and author, she shares her relatable and heartfelt messages with others who want to awaken to their true greatness and experience lasting happiness. This is her first book.

For more information, please visit JudiMiller.net

Made in the USA
Middletown, DE
09 August 2020